$$t = \frac{\overline{X}_1 - \overline{X}_2}{\sqrt{\dfrac{Sp^2}{n_1} + \dfrac{Sp^2}{n_2}}}$$

Making Sense of Research

A Guide to for Compleme ..... hers

Martha Brown Menard, PhD, CMT

Many thanks to the following journals for permission to reprint studies:

1. *Journal of the American Medical Association*: Trends in Alternative Medicine Use in the United States, 1990-1997. Results of a Follow-up National Survey
2. *Applied Nursing Research*: The Effect of Massage on Pain in Cancer Patients
3. *Obstetrics & Gynecology*: Randomized Controlled Study of Premenstrual Symptoms Treated With Ear, Hand, and Foot Reflexology
4. *Journal of Advanced Nursing*: Mastectomy, Body Image and Therapeutic Massage: A Qualitative Study of Women's Experience

The quotes at the beginning of each chapter are by Sir Peter Medawar, from his book Advice to a Young Scientist.

If you have comments or suggestions for improving subsequent editions of this book, please email them to Martha Brown Menard at: marthamenard@earthlink.net.

Making Sense of Research
Martha Brown Menard, PhD, CMT.
© Copyright 2003

To order copies, please contact:
Curties-Overzet Publications Inc.
330 Dupont Street, Suite 400
Toronto, Ontario
Canada M5R 1V9
Toll Free Phone: 1-888-649-5411
Fax: 416-923-8116
Website: www.curties-overset.com
E-mail: info@curties-overzet.com

ISBN 978-0-9685256-3-0

Acknowledgements

For Nathaniel
There is no difference between giving and receiving.

No one writes a book alone. Many people have contributed to the writing of this volume. Thanks first to publisher and colleague Debra Curties, who initially approached me about turning a continuing education workshop into book form. Debra has also been a terrific editor to work with; I appreciate her endless patience with someone new to this process.

To all the teachers over the years who have made science exciting: Paul Lyle (chemistry); Carolyn Bruner (biology); Ron MacVittie, who managed to make math interesting; John Walsh, who taught me anatomy and physiology; Sue Colletta and Ray Bratton (chemistry); and especially Barry Hinton (gross anatomy) and Bruce Gansneder (research methods). Thanks to Don Ball for demystifying statistics and suggesting that I consider a degree in educational research. A special thanks to Peyton Taylor, MD, and Doug DeGood, PhD, who facilitated my dissertation research at UVA.

To my all my clients, who have always been my greatest teachers and who were forbearing when I needed to take time away from my practice to write. To all my close friends, who were so supportive of me during this process, especially Brooke Persons, John Boyer, Evan Boyer, Michael Crear, and Charlotte and David Hisey.

To the people who read and contributed suggestions to the manuscript, thanks for your tremendous help in improving and polishing the text: Peter Becker, Allan Best, Stephen Cormier, Trish Dryden, Paul Finch, Glenn Hymel, Janet Kahn, Brian Menard, Jan Schwartz, and Roger Tolle.

Table of Contents

Foreword

by Allan Best, Ph.D.

Senior Scientist, Centre for Clinical Epidemiology and Evaluation, Vancouver Hospital and Health Sciences Centre; Clinical Professor, Health Care and Epidemiology, University of British Columbia

The world is changing, and health care with it. We're on the threshold of a new age—evidence-based medicine—and it is increasingly important that both complementary and conventional practitioners become comfortable in this arena. Indeed, it is to be hoped that we are moving towards a new view of care—integrative care—that weaves together the best of conventional and complementary traditions. In this paradigm shift, evidence-based medicine can provide a common ground, a shared language for practitioners from different traditions to learn to work together.

The world is changing in other ways too, as consumers want to be more active and collaborative in their care. They want the facts so they can judge for themselves. All practitioners—complementary and conventional—find themselves on the hot seat to make sense of often conflicting claims. The demand is for better facts, more discernment, and a fair balance among care options. This demand will only grow as the baby boomers face more age-related and chronic diseases, where there are few easy answers or magic bullets, and want more integrative, person-centred, compassionate, and balanced care models.

The mushrooming use of the Internet and other knowledge management tools creates a window of opportunity for complementary practitioners to get in on the ground floor. What will this look like? Clients increasingly will do their homework before a visit to a practitioner. They will know that there are prevention and treatment options involving both conventional and complementary modalities. It will become important for practitioners to have a working knowledge of both good and bad information on the Internet, and of the strengths and limitations of a wide range of practitioner and product options. In exchange for the gift of collaborative decision-making, complementary practitioners will learn new ways of practicing that genuinely place the client at the center of person-centred care, with a team of professionals who work synergistically to manage care efficiently and effectively. We'll see a coming together of complementary and behavioral medicine, tapping into research advances on self-directed learning, lifestyle change, and self management of chronic disease. The practitioner role will shift significantly, beyond caregiver to health partner, coach, and fellow learner. It's an exciting (and inevitable) vision, but one that moves us all into unexplored territory.

What will be your role in this changing landscape? For some, it will mean doing more reading to see what the latest research says—keeping up to date. Frankly, I hope that many of you find this a little frustrating as you become more aware of just how much new research is coming out, and how hard it is to make sense of it all and stay current. From that frustration can grow deepened resolve to be an effective guide for your clients as they make tough decisions. You'll need to sharpen your research literacy so that you can discern what to trust and what to question. You'll need to develop strategies for using your scarce time and energy in a personal plan for continuous learning about evidence-based care. Finally, a growing number of you will get hooked by the importance of this vision of integrated, evidence-based practice, and get involved in doing research. Some of you will seek out formal courses, and others will explore ways of becoming a collaborating practitioner, pooling practice data to learn from shared experience. The path towards the vision is a journey, and you'll find your own way as you go. This book provides a doorway through which to begin.

Dr. Menard speaks with wisdom and authority, showing how the highfalutin language of researchers actually makes sense! She clearly and simply shines a light on why research literacy is a key skill for complementary practitioners as they increasingly play their part in integrative client care. An informed reading of the evidence and appropriate scepticism about the art of the possible can only make us better providers; we owe it to our clients, our professions, and ourselves. This book offers the tools and disciplines we all need to meet that challenge.

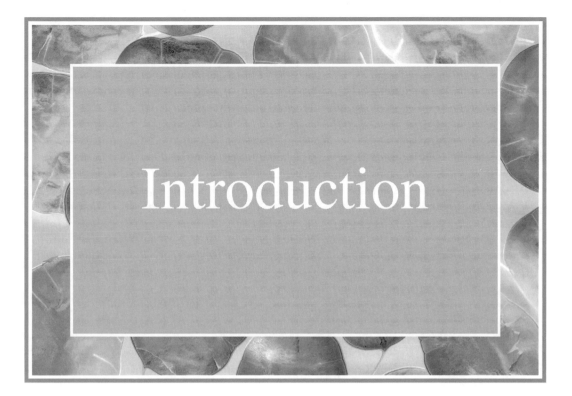

Introduction

The beginner must read, but intently and choosily and not too much.

P. B. Medawar

Why I Wrote This Book

I believe that reading research offers every complementary practitioner a valuable tool for improving the quality of care you are able to offer your clients, and for ensuring that you and your loved ones receive the best possible health care. Understanding research is vital to the continued development of complementary therapies. Yet it remains a critical gap in the professional education of many practitioners.

When I graduated from massage school in 1982, research was the farthest thing from my mind. I was more concerned with getting my practice off the ground and working as a teaching assistant. Although the training I received was excellent, I realized after a few months of private practice and keeping up with students' questions that there was much more to learn, and decided to go back to college to complete my undergraduate degree.

Despite a wonderfully eclectic academic program that allowed me to combine courses in gross anatomy, physiology, and biochemistry with others in psychology and athletic training, after a few more years of practice I found myself still dissatisfied with my level of knowledge. I began to read medical, nursing, and psychology journal articles about massage therapy, searching to find the relatively few that appeared in the health care literature at that time.

At first, I was pleased to find any research and interpreted any study that had positive findings as proof that massage really worked. However, as I carefully read more studies with both negative and positive results, I realized that the reality was more complex. It also seemed to me that many studies were designed by people who knew very little about the actual practice of massage therapy. The more I read, the more I thought I could develop a study that would reflect a more accurate assessment of what massage could do in a given situation.

In 1992, I entered the graduate clinical psychology program at the University of Virginia knowing that I wanted to design a study evaluating some aspect of massage therapy for my master's thesis. It was an auspicious time to become involved in massage therapy research. In the same year that I enrolled in graduate school, Dr. Tiffany Field opened the Touch Research Institute at the University of Miami, the US Congress had recently created the Office of Alternative Medicine* as part of the National Institutes of Health, and the American Massage Therapy Association developed the AMTA Foundation to sponsor research on massage therapy.

Through discussions with professors and fellow students, I learned more about how to read journal articles critically. I realized that some of the studies I had been reading had other problems besides the massage protocols. Understanding the logic behind design features such as blinding and random assignment, and understanding how they increased or undermined credibility in other research studies helped me in developing my own. In many ways, this book is the one I wish had been available to me when I was a student.

I went on to complete my Ph.D. in education, specifically in research methods, the theory and practice of how to design and conduct research. The study I designed for my thesis on the effect of massage on postoperative outcomes was among the first projects to be funded by the new Office of Alternative Medicine. It became my doctoral dissertation.[1] With the experience gained from conducting my own study, I began speaking to other massage practitioners in the United States and Canada about my work and about research in general.

Many of the practitioners I spoke with were excited about research and its potential to help massage therapy become more accepted within the larger health care field. But without any background or training, most seemed to feel that research was something mysterious, difficult, and

---

* Now upgraded to the National Center for Complementary and Alternative Medicine or NCCAM.

almost impossible for the average massage therapist or other complementary practitioner to understand. Motivated by these conversations, I began teaching workshops on how to read a clinical research article. This book developed from the material presented at these workshops, and has been expanded and updated to provide a thorough introduction to the topic. Through it, I hope to convey a necessary and important skill to a wider audience than I could ever expect to reach in person.

Why Does Research Literacy Matter?

Why do I think research literacy is important? First, research is a fundamental aspect of each of the conventional health care disciplines: medicine, nursing, psychology, physical therapy, speech therapy, occupational therapy, and so on. Research supports the theoretical foundation of a discipline and helps to distinguish useful treatments and practices from those that offer no benefit or prove harmful to patients. In addition, other complementary therapies such as chiropractic and acupuncture have developed a sizable body of research to support their use. This has helped facilitate their acceptance by conventional medicine and the general public.

Key to this acceptance is the effort to reduce the language barrier between conventional medicine and complementary approaches to health. As complementary practitioners we are in the minority within the larger health care field, and it is particularly important that we be able to explain our work in terms that others can grasp. Understanding research greatly improves our ability to communicate effectively with other health care professionals through a shared frame of reference and a common language.

Next, being able to locate and critically evaluate research in one's field is essential to providing the best possible care for clients. Reading research is one way to stay current on the latest developments, and it can be part of what keeps the work intellectually stimulating. Because news about recent research is often reported in the popular media, clients or other health care providers may approach practitioners with questions about what implications a new study might have. A good example is the controversial study claiming to debunk Therapeutic Touch that was designed and conducted by a nine year old and published in the Journal of the American Medical Association in 1998.[2] Although the methods used in the study appear rigorous at first glance, closer examination reveals that the procedure used to test the practitioners' ability to detect the subtle energy field bears little resemblance to the way in which Therapeutic Touch is practiced. It is incumbent upon practitioners to be able to discuss questions that arise from research in their field. Understanding how to evaluate research findings helps one to do this knowledgeably, with ease and confidence.

Finally, research is increasingly important for all of us as consumers in the health care system. As patients, we are beginning to assume a more active role in the health care partnership; more of us are seeking out research studies for the most current information about our own care. Popular media often do not report study findings in enough detail to determine how much confidence to place in the results or whether they apply to particular groups such as women or minorities. The media are also more likely to emphasize the most newsworthy angle instead of the usually more cautious interpretation found in peer-reviewed journals. Understanding research may be important to all of us at some point in helping us ask doctors the right questions to make sure that we and those close to us get the best possible care.

Goals of This Book

This book was written to help make research more accessible to all who are interested, especially those without a background or training in science. As massage and other complementary therapies become more integrated into conventional health care, it is increasingly necessary that we become research literate. Although this book was written to fill a critical gap in the education of massage therapists, any complementary practitioner or interested layperson will find the concepts and skills presented here useful. To this end, I have tried as much as possible to write in plain English, keeping technical terms to a minimum and providing clear explanations where needed. A glossary is also provided for easy reference.

The primary goal of this book is to increase your ability to locate and evaluate relevant research articles to enhance your work and your health. As you become more proficient, you will likely find yourself becoming a bit more skeptical about accepting what you read at face value. You will also notice yourself honing your critical thinking skills. For those who may be interested in actively participating in research in some capacity, this book introduces basic concepts as a foundation for further education. One of the best ways to learn how to conduct research is to read the findings of other investigators and study their successes and mistakes. Reading research gives you a feel for how scientists think. In addition, critically reviewing and integrating existing research on a topic is a necessary first step in designing any study.

As I said at the beginning of this introduction, I believe research literacy is a useful tool that can improve the quality of care practitioners are able to offer clients. A major result of becoming research literate is the enhancement of your knowledge and professional skills, for example, in developing treatment plans and in communicating more effectively with other health care providers. Becoming research literate creates a basis for improved clinical decision-making, successful outcomes for your clients, and increased professional recognition. Simply put, understanding research can help you become a better practitioner.

How to Use This Book

The book is structured so that the reader begins with a broad perspective on understanding research and then progresses to more specific aspects. General concepts, including the underlying assumptions of scientific research, are introduced first. Next, different types of research studies are identified and their strengths and weaknesses described. The various sections of a journal article and how to read them critically are then outlined in detail. Following this discussion, four studies are provided as examples of how to evaluate a journal article, using a question and answer format. To assist the reader, I have also listed learning objectives at the beginning of each chapter and provided questions or activities to reinforce knowledge and enhance skills at the end of most chapters.

My hope for every practitioner who uses this book is that the knowledge and skills gained as a result will create a platform for greater confidence in your ability to understand and use research, and lead to increased professional success. May this book help you continue a lifelong commitment to learning, caring, and excellence in your chosen field. I wish you the very best.

Let the beauty we love be what we do.
There are hundreds of ways to kneel and kiss the ground.

Rumi

References

1. Menard MB. *The Effect of Massage Therapy on Post Surgical Outcomes* [*dissertation*]. Charlottesville: University of Virginia; 1995.

2. Rosa L, Rosa E, Sarner L, Barrett S. **A Close Look at Therapeutic Touch**. *Journal of the American Medical Association.* 1998; 239(13): 1005-1010.

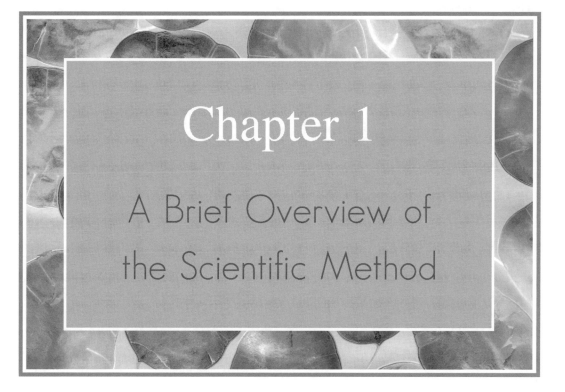

Chapter 1

A Brief Overview of the Scientific Method

"The scientific method,"
as it is sometimes called, is a potentiation of common sense.

P. B. Medawar

Learning Objectives

- Know the bases upon which knowledge claims can be made.

- Understand the concepts of falsification and reproducibility.

- Describe the differences between quantitative and qualitative methods.

- Differentiate among internal, external, and statistical validity.

- Identify four threats to internal validity.

- Describe how design considerations such as random assignment are used to increase the credibility of a study.

Before one begins reading journal articles and evaluating their merits, it is helpful to understand some basic concepts about the processes involved in scientific research. This chapter introduces these fundamental ideas and provides an overview of the underlying and often unspoken assumptions about how science is practiced. Concepts necessary to critically evaluate research studies are also introduced in this chapter.

Science as a Way of Thinking

When people hear the word "science," various types of images come to mind. Associations with science can be positive or negative, depending on how it is portrayed in the popular media or based on personal experiences with education. A different way to think about science may be to simply consider it as a way of looking at the world with a spirit of open-minded curiosity and inquiry.

Science is not, however, the only way of seeking or gaining knowledge about the world. Claims about knowledge may be made on other grounds such as tradition, intuition, or authority. For example, we may have learned that a familiar procedure should be performed in a certain manner because it has always been done that way. We might feel that a person we are being introduced to is untrustworthy because we 'just know it.' Or we may have been taught that massage is contraindicated for people with cancer because our teacher and Dr. J. H. Kellogg said so. In some circumstances, all of these methods for accepting knowledge may be valid. But there are two other methods, rationalism and empiricism, which have their foundations respectively in critical thinking and sensory experience.

Rationalism is a way of acquiring knowledge through the use of reason or logic. A classic example of a logical deduction is the following argument:

All men are mortal. (premise)
Socrates is a man. (premise)
Therefore Socrates is mortal. (conclusion)

There is one problem with this approach: the conclusion is valid only when the premises are accurate. In the example above, the reader has no way to independently verify that Socrates is really a man and not the name of a fishing boat or a software program. Without some way to assess the accuracy of a premise, both it and any resulting conclusion are based on assumption alone. To have more confidence in the results of this process, each step must be tested.

Empiricism is a way of acquiring knowledge through objective evaluation. An empiricist accepts a statement as true only if he or she can demonstrate it through physical measurement. Something cannot exist, nor can a statement be true unless it can be quantified through the senses. This method of gaining knowledge requires observation and analysis, and provides a way to test the premises and conclusions of rationalism. Science creates the basis for knowledge claims by marrying the rational and empirical approaches. It seeks to validate the assumptions of rationalism through careful observation, assessment, and evaluation of empirical or sensory information. This way of thinking defines science and scientific research.

Above all, scientific research is about asking questions. "What," "how," and "why" are questions scientists often ask about the natural world. They look to get their answers through the testing of hypotheses. A **hypothesis** is a highly specific statement that can be demonstrated to be true or false through the methodical gathering and analysis of empirical information or data. The different methods used to conduct scientific investigation through testing hypotheses will be discussed later in this chapter and also in Chapter 3.

An essential feature of almost every research question is that it seeks to describe or explain relationships between variables. For example, pollsters may want to know how men and women plan to vote on an issue; teachers may want to know if different teaching methods can improve reading comprehension; or physicians may want to know whether a new treatment has any effect on a chronic illness.

Another aspect of science is that it is systematic. Once a hypothesis is identified, information or data related to it is gathered in a methodical way. The researcher attempts to ensure that no relevant information is overlooked or left out, whether from personal preference or just plain forgetfulness. Particularly at the beginning stages of a scientific inquiry, no one knows what observation or piece of data may prove to be important. If the information collected can be expressed in numerical form, a systematic approach often includes the use of statistical calculations to determine whether there are any changes among the variables or outcomes being studied and, if so, whether these results could have occurred due to chance alone.

Science also has an antiauthoritarian element. As suggested earlier, part of the essence of science is not taking someone else's word for it. Rather than relying on history, opinion, the experience of others, or individual desire that a hypothesis be true or false, science accepts an assertion that something is true based on evidence. Peer-reviewed journals, where scientific articles are published after an evaluation by colleagues and experts in the researcher's field, allow for sharing study results and their implications with a wider audience. Readers are free to make up their own minds about the worth and credibility of the author's methods, results, and conclusions.

There is a growing trend toward evidence-based medicine in health care today; both new and established treatments are expected to demonstrate their effectiveness based on research. Evidence-based medicine requires the application of scientific method to the practices of the health care professions, and poses a challenge for both conventional and complementary practitioners.

Falsification and Accumulation of Knowledge

Falsification is an idea first put forth by the philosopher Karl Popper.[1] It can be summarized as follows: because it is always possible that new information could be discovered at any time, even about a research question that seems to have been thoroughly investigated, we can never say that "such and such is certainly true." We can only say that a hypothesis is tentatively true to date because no evidence to disconfirm it has come to light. Popper's view is that rather than working towards verification, that is, demonstrating a thing to be true, science works best when attempting to prove it false. When a hypothesis fails to be demonstrated as false enough times, it becomes part of accepted knowledge. However, the idea of falsification implies that this status is always provisional and that there are degrees of certainty. Lee Cronbach[2] may have put it best when he described the pursuit of scientific knowledge as "reducing uncertainty."

In this way, although errors and mistakes may be accepted for a time, science is essentially self-correcting because it is always open to new information. As new information becomes available, accepted knowledge eventually changes to accommodate and include it. Sometimes this assimilation takes place over a long time, particularly if the new information stands in contradiction to previously held beliefs, but if the evidence is strong enough it will eventually become integrated into the body of accepted knowledge.*

From this perspective, you can also see that one study alone rarely provides enough information or evidence to conclusively answer a question. It is much more common for a body of evidence to accumulate gradually over time. One study builds upon another. This is what Einstein meant when he said, "If I have seen farther than other men, it is because I have stood on the shoulders of giants." As more studies are conducted and more information becomes available, a more complete and detailed picture is formed.

Reproducibility of Results

Reproducibility refers to the capacity of a study to be repeated, preferably by a different investigator, and to produce the same or similar enough results. Another type of replication can be found in studies that build upon previous work. Reproducibility adds greatly to the credibility or trustworthiness of scientific evidence; it is the ultimate standard in terms of validating a hypothesis. Experimental results that cannot be reproduced by others using the same methods and materials are viewed skeptically by the scientific community. Repeated failure to reproduce results under reasonably similar conditions is usually considered evidence of disconfirmation. A standard practice in reporting research results is to give sufficient detail for a fellow scientist to reproduce the study.

---

* *The amount of time necessary is sometimes a generation or more, as younger scientists who may be more open to new ideas come up through the ranks. There is a well-known ironic saying acknowledging the social and cultural nature of scientific revolutions: "Science progresses one death at a time."*

Making Sense of Research

Science as a Social Activity

Science takes place via human interaction, through informal communication among colleagues with similar interests, more formal presentations and discussions at conferences, and publication of completed research findings in peer-reviewed journals. Knowledge-building is a social process as much as a scientific one.

Because human beings are fallible, the social norms of science help to minimize the presence of bias in the processes through which speculation becomes knowledge. These norms include an expectation of integrity in the design, conduct, interpretation, and publication of research studies. One example is the practice among peer-reviewed journals of requiring disclosure of all sources of financial support for a study, so that readers can judge the possibility or extent to which the study may be biased because of who funded the research. A study concluding that smoking poses no substantial health risks in spite of numerous contradictory studies would be viewed even more suspiciously if it were funded by the Tobacco Institute.

The philosopher of science Thomas Kuhn[3] articulated the idea that scientific world views or paradigms define the kinds of research questions that may legitimately be asked. What is thought to be 'legitimate' can vary according to the social norms and the assumptions of a culture and what is considered within that culture to be useful or important knowledge. Other writers since Kuhn have detailed ways in which the practice of science has sometimes been distorted by cultural biases, such as the idea that women[4] or people of color[5] are somehow inferior to white males.

Quantitative and Qualitative Methods

In the traditional scientific world view, hypotheses are premised on the assumption that there is a uniform reality that can be observed, measured, and expressed in terms of numbers. There is also an assumption of linear cause and effect, for example, that a certain treatment causes a specific result. Methods for investigating research questions based on these assumptions are called **quantitative methods**. Their essence is the testing of hypotheses, starting from deductive reasoning or theories, and using numbers as a kind of shorthand to summarize and manage large amounts of information.

In the quantitative approach, the researcher manipulates the treatment setting and the participants in the study, controlling as much of the environment as possible. Elements of research design are employed to rule out rival explanations of the results in order that the treatment alone can be claimed to have caused them. Statistical analysis is then used to show the probability that the results could have occurred by chance. A low probability means that the odds of the results occurring by chance alone are unlikely. A major assumption is that results obtained in one setting should be reproducible under the same conditions in another.

Qualitative methods are generally based on a different set of assumptions from quantitative methods. In the qualitative world view there is no distinction between the observer and what is observed - each affects the other and is part of an ongoing process of change. The observer can describe what he or she observes, but there is no assumption of a single external reality, and any description is seen as only one of several realities that may be equally valid. Rather than a single, linear cause and effect, there may be multiple causes or factors that influence outcomes. Each situation is considered unique. Another hallmark of qualitative research is the importance placed on observation of phenomena in their natural settings and on the personal contact and insights of the researcher in relation to the participants in the study, rather than a more laboratory-like manipulation of the research setting.

Qualitative methods consist of three types of data collection: open-ended interviews, direct observation, and documents such as personal journals, correspondence, or answers to open-ended questionnaires and surveys. These types of data collection encompass a variety of applications across many fields. For example, open-ended interviews are used in focus groups, where participants may be asked to discuss their thoughts, perceptions, and feelings regarding consumer products or political issues. Observations can be made along a continuum, from the perspective of an outsider to a group or activity such as the work of chimpanzee biologist Jane Goodall, to the perspective of a full participant as in Gloria Steinem's description of her career as a Playboy bunny. Documents ranging from the letters and diaries of historical figures to postings on an Internet bulletin board can all be analyzed for themes and trends.

The qualitative view in some ways is a more holistic perspective. Its essence is the desire to understand complex systems, and to explore and pursue new paths of discovery as they emerge.

• Which Method is Better?

The choice of methods in research is still somewhat contentious, although less so now than a generation ago. For many years a great divide separated quantitative and qualitative researchers, with each touting the advantages of their preferred methodology while stressing the limitations of the other's. The quantitative paradigm predominates in health care research. The biological sciences have long tried to base their methods on the rigorous ones used in hard sciences like classical physics and chemistry. In recent years, however, there has been a greater openness to the qualitative philosophy in health care research, particularly in nursing. Studies in the disciplines of sociology, anthropology, psychology, and education often employ qualitative methods. The incorporation of such methods, and the types of knowledge gained as a result, have much to offer the study of health care.

Both quantitative and qualitative studies require careful planning and preparation in order to yield useful results. Although qualitative methods developed at least partially out of dissatisfaction with the limits of quantitative methods, in many ways the qualitative philosophy has always been part of the foundation of science. Research hypotheses are often developed based on detailed description and observation from the field. It is not a simple either-or question.

Studies may use elements of both approaches. Usually it is a matter of appropriateness given the research question being asked. In an exploratory or pilot study, qualitative methods may be employed to describe and to attempt to understand phenomena, collecting more information because there is not yet enough to form a highly specific and quantifiable hypothesis. Such a study may be used to build a theory rather than to verify it. For example, in a study of smoking behavior, researchers might use a focus group in the development of the survey questionnaire. Quantitative data may also be collected as part of a study and can be used to illuminate patterns that might otherwise be overlooked. In a program evaluation of a massage therapy school, for example, job placement rates would be considered necessary information.

The double-blind randomized clinical trial - the 'gold standard' of the quantitative approach - is usually based on a body of accumulated information, enough so that a theory has been developed and is now ready to be tested. In this type of study, qualitative data may also be collected to document factors that may have influenced the results, or to gather information that could be useful in implementing the treatment in another setting. Unusual events or unanticipated consequences can be described and used to generate or refine new hypotheses to be tested, as in the observation of Kaposi's sarcoma incidence in young men leading to the identification of AIDS.

Well-designed research always uses the methodology most appropriate to the question being asked. Sometimes a strategic combination of quantitative and qualitative methods is the best solution. Each method requires rigorous planning and implementation; qualitative methods cannot be applied as a solution to a poorly designed quantitative study, and vice versa.

Qualitative and quantitative methods both assess the credibility or trustworthiness of a study based on the reliability and validity of the evidence as it is presented and interpreted. Even though the methodologies are quite different from each other, the underlying logic used in evaluating either quantitative or qualitative studies is the same. Most of the emphasis in this book is placed on studies using quantitative methods, because these are used more extensively in health care research.

Basic Concepts Involved in Evaluating Research

The primary purpose in conducting a study is to be able to draw conclusions about the nature of the relationships between variables studied, such as treatment and outcome. In evaluating the credibility of any research study there are two major concerns. The first is with the capacity of the findings to be generalized to a larger group than the one that participated in the study. This is known as **external validity**. A common example of this concern is found in medical research involving animals, which raises the question of the degree to which a particular study's results can be applied to humans. Also, studies that focus on a narrow range of participants or subjects may have more limited generalizability than studies that include a more diverse group.

The second major concern is "the capacity of the study to link cause and effect,"[6] known as **internal validity**. Studies with good internal validity should exclude other hypotheses as plausible alternative explanations for their findings. For example, let's say that you are reading a study proposing that dogs are telepathic.[7] The outcome being measured to demonstrate a dog's telepathic ability is the time at which the dog goes to the door to wait for its owner after he or she has decided to return home. To have good internal validity, the study's design should rule out plausible alternative explanations, for example that the dog's seemingly telepathic behavior might be a response to a familiar routine. In Rupert Sheldrake's experiments testing this hypothesis, he gave the dog's owner a pager and signaled him or her to come home at randomly selected times, so that designated time of return was not known until the pager went off. He used a video camera with a time stamp to verify when the dog went to the door to wait. Sheldrake also had the owner randomly vary the means of transportation home, sometimes walking or taking a subway or bus.

Threats to Internal Validity

Flaws in the design of a study can threaten its internal validity and weaken its credibility. Cook and Campbell[8] have described a number of threats to internal validity common in research design. These are summarized below and should be kept in mind as you read and evaluate the study examples given later in this book. Certain types of studies are better than others at ruling out particular threats to validity; this aspect will be discussed in more detail in Chapter 3. Design features that help to promote credibility are discussed later in this chapter.

Threats to internal validity are sometimes referred to as **confounds** or **sources of bias**. A confounding variable blurs or masks the effect of another variable. For example, age may affect motor performance as much as an intervention being tested. Bias, in the research sense, refers to a situation where there is systematic error in the measurement of a variable, such as the tendency to underestimate the impact of the placebo effect in treatment outcomes.

• *History*

History in this context is defined as an event that occurs during the course of the study and influences the outcome but is unrelated to the treatment or intervention. For example, you are reading a study testing a new treatment for depression. The participants in the study are college students at a major university. The treatment is administered over spring break, and many of the students in the study start new relationships during that time. How do you think falling in love would affect the students' reports of how depressed they feel? Under such circumstances, the new treatment would likely appear to be much more effective than it actually is.

- *Maturation*

Maturation refers to events that occur naturally with the passage of time. Children get stronger as they grow older; a person performing repetitions with weights becomes more fatigued the longer he or she works out; a surgical patient reports less pain as the incision heals. In medicine, this is sometimes referred to as natural history or the natural course of a process or disease. One way to rule out maturation as an explanation for a study's results is to use a comparison or control group that does not receive the intervention or treatment.

- *Testing*

Testing refers to learned responses, such as participants becoming familiar with a process or instrument used more than once to measure an outcome of interest. The more often a test is given, the more familiar the participant can become with the correct response, or be inclined to recall particular items or mistakes when tested again. This is the reason that a test like the Scholastic Achievement Test (SAT), which is used to assess a student's academic ability, limits the number of times a person can take the test.

- *Instrumentation*

Instrumentation as a threat to validity occurs where there is a change or problem with the degree of measurement possible with a given instrument. For example, human observers become more experienced over time and are thus able to discriminate smaller or finer differences at the end of a study compared to the beginning. Conversely, observers may become fatigued and less able to make consistent judgments. Instrumentation is sometimes referred to as instrument decay.

Another type of instrumentation problem is called a ceiling or floor effect, where the instrument cannot measure something above or below its scale. For example, a ceiling effect occurs when a test fails to measure the IQ of an extremely intelligent person because the test or instrument scale does not go high enough.

- *Regression*

Many studies use some variation of the before-and-after treatment design, where participants are measured before an intervention and then again afterward. Regression, sometimes called **regression to the mean**, describes the tendency of very high or very low baseline (initial) measurements to average out by the end of a study. For example, in studies of method effectiveness in teaching reading, groups of disadvantaged children often show marked improvement. This may attest to the degree to which they were disadvantaged at the outset rather than the efficacy of the specific teaching method. In the context of assessing therapeutic effectiveness, this threat to validity would tend to make a treatment appear more effective than it actually is because the difference between the baseline measurement and the ending measurements appears larger. If the instrument used to measure the outcome is unreliable, the scores will vary even more and the effect of regression will be larger still.

- *Selection*

Selection is one of the most important and sometimes subtle threats to validity. Perhaps a public opinion firm decides to conduct a survey to find out how extensive altruistic behavior is in urban populations, and, for the sake of convenience, polls people at a holistic health fair. The same factor that makes people interested in holistic health may also make them more likely to behave in altruistic ways, including volunteering to answer the pollster's questions. Selection bias also occurs when two groups are chosen that differ from each other in some significant way, are both given an intervention or treatment, and are then compared to each other. Any effect observed may be a result of the difference between the groups rather than the treatment they receive.

- *Mortality*

Mortality in the research sense refers to attrition, or the tendency for people to drop out or stop participating in research studies before the data collection is completed. Attrition can introduce selection bias by making the group different at the end of data collection than it was at the beginning. For example, a new drug for depression has such unpleasant side effects that people with the most severe depression (and therefore less tolerance of additional unpleasantness) tend to drop out of the study at a higher rate than those with less severe symptoms. Consequently, the remaining people then seem to demonstrate miraculous improvement because their symptoms were milder to begin with. As a result, the drug appears to be more effective than it really is.

Statistical Validity

Another concern, related to internal validity, that can arise when evaluating a study is its statistical validity. Statistical validity is closely related to internal validity, and generally refers to the "number-crunching" aspects of a research study - whether the numbers and the formulas used were properly computed, justified, and explained. Problems that can occur with the statistical validity of a research study include multiple comparisons and low statistical power, sometimes referred to as **Type I** and **Type II errors**.

In many of our examples of threats to internal validity, the result is that a treatment appears to have an effect when it actually does not. Falsely concluding that a genuine effect exists when it does not is a Type I error. Statistical tests are routinely performed on research data to rule out the possibility that seemingly meaningful results are actually due to chance. However, the more comparisons or statistical tests that are run on a given set of data, especially when several outcomes are measured, the greater the possibility that some differences will show up as statistically meaningful just by chance alone. Some statistical tests are designed to be used in cases where only one outcome is measured, while others are designed for the analysis of multiple outcomes. The type of statistical analysis used should make sense given the hypothesis being tested and the number of outcomes measured. More detailed information on recognizing statistical validity issues will be presented in Chapters 4 and 5.

Another problem arises when there are not enough participants in a study, also known as small sample size. A small number of participants means low statistical power. Here power refers to the ability of the statistical test to detect a genuine effect when one exists and is based on the number of participants and outcomes to be measured. Generally, the more participants who complete their role in a study and the fewer the outcomes measured, the higher the statistical power to detect a true effect. In a large high school, which survey of students voting in a student council election would you have more confidence in - one that asked 10 students or one that asked 100 students? If power is low, a true effect may be operating but cannot be demonstrated by the data. This is a Type II error: falsely concluding that no effect is present when one actually is. Another way to think of Type II error is the truism in science that absence of evidence is not evidence of absence.

Another problem related to statistical validity can occur when there is a lack of standardization of treatment. If a treatment is implemented in several different ways or formats by various research personnel, this can reduce the effectiveness of the treatment or make it more difficult to measure accurately, based on the assumption that the treatment should be the same for everyone. Lack of standardization usually introduces a larger amount of error in the data collected. This issue is especially relevant to research in complementary medicine and will be discussed in more detail in Chapter 6.

Other Design Considerations in Evaluating Research

Other design issues relevant to health care research include random assignment, blinding, placebo or nonspecific response, sham treatment, and model fit validity.

- *Random Assignment*

Random assignment to group is often used in studies to reduce the effect of potential influences over which the investigator has no control by ensuring that each participant has an equal chance of being assigned to a treatment or a control group. If a pool of participants is divided into two groups and one group is randomly assigned to receive a particular treatment while the other is designated the control group, chance variations in the treatment environment or lifestyle factors that could affect the outcome should be equal between the two groups, thus canceling each other out. Generally, random assignment to treatment increases the credibility of a study because it is very effective at ruling out other explanations, even those that the researcher cannot anticipate. But random assignment is not possible in every situation for both practical and ethical reasons.

Imagine a research study where participants were randomly assigned to receive a harmful treatment or to have a beneficial treatment withheld. No research ethics review committee* would approve it.

However, while the use of random assignment avoids many threats to internal validity, it is not a panacea for increasing the trustworthiness of a study. Random assignment does not address what are called **reactivity issues** in studies, which occur when participants react to the obtrusiveness of the study's data collection methods or when the normal conditions of the study are disrupted in some way, usually because participants figure out which group they are in. For example, **diffusion of treatment** may occur when people in the comparison group realize that they are not receiving the active treatment and attempt to obtain it on their own. Or, participants may try harder or feel depressed when they realize that they are receiving a less desirable treatment.

At other times randomization may fail during the course of a study. For example, participants might communicate with each other and compare notes, or systematic attrition can occur because one treatment is less desirable. Participants may seek out additional treatments and use these during the study without informing the researcher. Random assignment may also not be appropriate when practitioner intention or client expectation are part of the treatment, or when individualization of treatment, learning, or choice are necessary for maximum effectiveness, as in studies that evaluate education, psychotherapy, and many complementary therapies.

Sometimes randomization procedures are faulty. It is standard practice in research to base the random assignment on a table of random numbers and to check the data to make sure that the randomization procedures worked. As a further measure of the integrity of the study, demographic data is typically reported to show that the groups of participants are indeed comparable to one another.

• *Blinding*

Blinding refers to concealing the group assignment from the participants, the researcher, or both. It is used to rule out expectation as an alternate explanation for a treatment effect. It is often used in conjunction with a placebo. Without participants knowing which treatment they are receiving, either active or placebo, expectation should be equal in both groups. If only the researcher or the participant is blinded, it is referred to as a single blind study; if neither the researcher nor the participant knows which group is receiving the treatment, it is called a double blind study. Blinding poses an obvious challenge for complementary modalities that involve manual skills. Although it is impossible to use double blinding in a study of a hands-on therapy, the person who

---

* *These are called Institutional Review Boards (IRBs), and ideally act as ethics committees within the institution where the research takes place, to safeguard the human rights of and protect from abuse the people who participate in health care research. I say ideally because abuses do sometimes occur. For example, pharmaceutical companies have recently been criticized for conducting clinical trials in third world nations where protection of human rights is more lax.*

collects or assesses the data can be blinded. Just as random assignment can sometimes fail during a study, blinding can too. An investigator should check to see if blinding procedures worked or if participants were able to guess what group they were in.

•   *Placebo Response and Nonspecific Treatment Effects*

A placebo is traditionally a pharmacologically inert substance, such as a sugar pill, or a treatment that has no effect on the outcome of interest. The use of a placebo treatment group is another way to control for participant expectation. Much has been written about nonspecific response in medicine; some authors estimate that it may account for 30 to 80 per cent of response to treatment.[9] As you might guess, placebos were first used in drug studies. However, researchers were surprised to learn that some participants responded to these inactive compounds as though given the active drug, apparently from their expectation that the placebo would help.

Another term that is sometimes used synonymously with placebo response is **nonspecific response**, or nonspecific treatment effect. These are more accurate and less pejorative terms than placebo response. Nonspecific responses result from pervasive aspects of health care interventions such as patient and practitioner beliefs, attitudes, and expectations, the nature and quality of the therapeutic relationship, or the degree and kind of patient social support. Because the nature of the healing relationship is that patients expect to be helped and practitioners intend to help them, nonspecific treatment elements are present to some degree in any treatment.

Although nonspecific response is a physiologically active treatment in and of itself, in other words it can produce actual effects and from a clinical perspective be quite desirable, it has a negative connotation in research and is regarded as an alternative explanation to be ruled out, as "noise" rather than "signal." Nonspecific response presents a thorny problem in health care research for a variety of reasons, among them the unfortunately still pervasive idea that mind and body are separable.

There is an extensive literature on nonspecific response that cannot be summarized in such a brief introduction to this fascinating topic. However, it is important to emphasize several points about the use of controls for nonspecific response. According to many psychologists, patient expectation and learned responses do more to explain nonspecific effects of treatment than the belief that only certain types of people are likely to respond to a placebo. Research summarized by Patrick Wall[10] shows that nonspecific responses are stronger and more frequent in studies where the participants know that potent narcotics such as morphine are being tested as compared to non-narcotic medications like aspirin. In studies using a crossover design,* the placebo effect is stronger when

---

* *In a crossover design, two groups are used and each receives a different treatment. At some point during the study the two groups switch treatments, or cross over, and the results of each treatment are compared before and after the switch.*

the placebo is given second rather than first, again suggesting learned behavior by patients. In addition, research has determined that those who are likely to respond strongly to nonspecific aspects of treatment are most easily identified by asking what their expectations are rather than by assessing their personality traits.

The traditional assumption of placebo as noise rather than signal assumes that there is a true therapeutic effect that can be separated out. This may not always be possible because all active substances or treatments have their own nonspecific components. Teasing out the relative contributions of specific and nonspecific effects can be difficult. Wall makes a strong case that participants in trials are quite sensitive to subtle cues from researchers or data collectors who may be blinded as to group but still have a general knowledge of what the study is investigating (as likely do the participants, based on their informed consent to participate in the study). The results are that blind trials are rarely truly blind, and that nonspecific treatment effects are not always independent of 'true' treatment effect.

In some cases, a placebo control group is not the best comparison group in evaluating the efficacy of a treatment. If a 'gold standard' treatment exists for a particular condition, a trial comparing the new intervention to the standard treatment is more useful.

A related issue is nocebo effect, or the effect of negative expectations. Anticipatory nausea and vomiting in patients undergoing chemotherapy is one example. Practitioners also may give subtle cues indicating distress to participants in a research study if they are asked to give a treatment which they believe to be ineffective.

- *Sham Treatment*

Sham treatments are a variation of the placebo control designed to separate the specific effect of a treatment from nonspecific effects. They are considered somewhat controversial among complementary practitioners. When a sham treatment is given the assumption is made that there is no specific effect being produced. Yet in order for the sham treatment to be credible to the participant it must closely mimic the real thing, thus running the risk that some specific effect may indeed be produced.

A related problem is the possibility that some therapies may depend largely on nonspecific effects for their results. Does this make them less effective or less clinically useful?

It is fairly easy to devise sham treatments for machines such as electrical stimulation. The treatment can be made credible if the machine lights up or otherwise appears to be active even though no treatment is being delivered. Acupuncture provides an excellent example of the difficulty with sham treatment. The act of needling a point, even if it is not one that is relevant for the condition being treated, may have a specific effect that could influence the outcome. In addition, patients who have received genuine acupuncture quickly learn from the sensation of the needle whether the acupuncturist has hit the point or not, so that experienced patients assigned to a sham treatment group are not likely to remain blinded for very long.

Therapies such as massage and other forms of bodywork pose considerable challenges to efforts to create credible yet sufficiently inactive forms of sham treatment. In some cases, social touch, such as parent/baby contact, has been used as a control for the nonspecific effects of touch in studies of massage with premature infants.[11] Other strategies might use a type of touch that is either too light or too heavy to produce the intended result, or, as in the acupuncture example, the treatment might be applied to an area of the body that should have no effect on the outcome being measured. The problem with all of these is that an active treatment is being compared with one that is less active, but how much less active is unknown. The body is an integrated system; if you touch one part the whole body knows it. If both treatments are active to a close enough degree, there may appear to be no effect because no significant difference in the outcomes between the two groups will be apparent. Sham treatments also present ethical issues of providing an ineffective treatment to people needing help or withholding a treatment that the practitioner believes to be beneficial. Thus, the use of sham treatment is not always an ideal solution.

- *Model Fit Validity*

This is a design consideration first discussed by Claire Cassidy.[12] Model fit validity refers to the idea that the underlying assumptions or model of the research methods being used should match those of the therapy being studied. This is an issue in much of the research on complementary therapies.

Cassidy contends that lack of model fit is like using the rules of baseball to understand or explain football. For instance, in many complementary therapies patients/clients are encouraged to be active participants in their care and treatment is individualized to meet each person's needs. These two ideas run counter to the assumption in most quantitative health care research that patients are relatively passive and interchangeable recipients of treatment for the purposes of the study. Rather than maximizing effectiveness, lack of standardized treatment is perceived as a source of error. If a complementary treatment is significantly altered to fit the research model or is not allowed to be performed as defined by its practitioners, then the study is not a valid assessment of the treatment.

For example, in many studies of massage therapy, the term 'massage therapy' is not explicitly defined from a theoretical perspective. In the United States, definitions from both the American Massage Therapy Association[13] and the National Certification Board for Therapeutic Massage and Bodywork[14] state that a healing relationship is an essential part of the practice of massage therapy. Rarely, however, does the massage intervention in research studies include or imply 'healing relationship' as a necessary part of the treatment. In many of these studies, treatment is provided by individuals without specific massage therapy training or experience, using standardized protocols that bear little resemblance to the way massage is clinically practiced. Studies that do not define treatments as they are clinically practiced, either explicitly or implicitly, tend to ignore crucial aspects of treatment, are reductionistic, and are not an honest test of the treatment or intervention under investigation.

Rather than discounting or dismissing the nonspecific components of complementary therapies, these could instead be assessed to determine their relative contribution to the efficacy of the treatment as a whole. Such information has value because it can be used to improve the clinical success of other types of treatment as well. Treatments that produce their results primarily from nonspecific effects should not be immediately regarded as lacking efficacy, particularly if they reliably produce a positive clinical outcome at a lower cost with little or no risk of adverse effects compared to medication or surgery.

Summary

Scientific method is based on a spirit of open-minded curiosity and inquiry, using applied common sense and systematic procedures. Knowledge is based on evidence, which accumulates over time as one study builds upon another. Science is also a social endeavor, and depends upon the integrity of the individuals who design, conduct, interpret, and publish research.

Two major types of methods used in research are quantitative and qualitative; each has a different set of underlying assumptions. Basic concepts involved in evaluating the credibility of research include external, internal, and statistical validity. Threats to validity, or bias, such as selection and maturation, can undermine the credibility of a study and reduce the capacity to draw definite conclusions from its results. Related issues such as the use of random assignment or control or comparison groups should be evaluated carefully in the context of the study to decide whether these have been used appropriately given the hypothesis being tested.

References

1. Popper KR. *The Logic of Scientific Discovery*. New York: Basic Books; 1959.

2. Cronbach LJ. *Designing Evaluations of Educational and Social Programs*. San Francisco: Jossey-Bass; 1982.

3. Kuhn TS. *The Structure of Scientific Revolutions (3rd edition)*. Chicago: University of Chicago Press; 1996.

4. Tavris C. *The Mismeasure of Woman*. New York: Simon and Schuster; 1992.

5. Gould SJ. *The Mismeasure of Man*. New York: W.W. Norton and Company; 1981.

6. Krathwohl DR. *Methods of Educational and Social Science Research*. New York: Longman Publishing Group; 1993.

7. Sheldrake R. *Dogs That Know When Their Owners are Coming Home*. New York: Three Rivers Press; 1999.

8. Cook TD, Campbell DT. *Quasi-experimentation: Design and Analysis for Field Settings*. Boston: Houghton Mifflin Company; 1979.

9. Moerman D. et al. **Placebo Effects and Research in Alternative and Conventional Medicine**. *Chinese Journal of Integrated Traditional and Western Medicine*. 1996; 2(2): 141-148.

10. Wall P. **The Placebo and Placebo Response**. In P. Wall and R. Melzack (eds.), *Textbook of Pain*. Edinburgh: Churchill Livingstone. 1994: 1297-1308.

11. Scafidi F. et al. **Massage Stimulates Growth in Preterm Infants: A Replication**. *Infant Behavior and Development*. 1990; 13: 167-188.

12. Cassidy C. **Unraveling the Ball of String: Reality, Paradigms and the Study of Alternative Medicine**. *Advances, The Journal of Mind-Body Medicine*. 1994; 10: 5-31.

13. American Massage Therapy Association. **AMTA Definition of Massage Therapy**. *www.amtamassage.org/about/definition.html*. Accessed February 3, 2000.

14. National Certification Board for Therapeutic Massage and Bodywork, *Background Information for NCBTMB's New Exam Content*. McLean, Virginia: National Certification Board for Therapeutic Massage and Bodywork; 1997.

Exercises

1. How do rationalism and empiricism work together in scientific research to reinforce the validity of knowledge claims?

2. Explain what is meant by the term 'falsificationism.'

3. What are some of the major ways in which qualitative and quantitative research methods differ from each other?

4. What is internal validity? Statistical validity?

5. Name three threats to internal validity.

6. What are nonspecific treatment effects?

7. How does the use of random assignment to group increase the internal validity of a study?

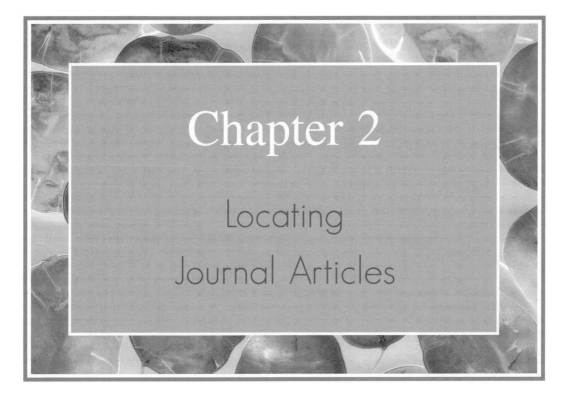

Chapter 2

Locating Journal Articles

We always need to know and understand a great deal more than we do already and to master many more skills than we now possess.

P. B. Medawar

Learning Objectives

- Understand the terms *field*, *keywords*, and *search strategy*.

- Perform a search for journal articles using PubMed.

- Save a search strategy using Cubby.

- Investigate other websites as additional resources for finding articles of interest.

There are numerous ways, both formal and informal, to locate journal articles or reports of research studies. For our purposes, we will concentrate on using publicly available computerized reference databases, as these are the most easily accessed by the largest number of readers. One database in particular, PubMed, will be discussed in detail. PubMed is the publicly available version of MEDLINE, the reference database maintained by the National Library of Medicine in Bethesda, Maryland. This database is very easy to use; you just point the mouse and click. Although we will focus on learning how to conduct a search specifically using PubMed, the same general principles apply to searching most computerized databases.

This chapter will make more sense if you sit down at a computer and use the information to simultaneously walk through a search. I have assumed minimal familiarity with computerized database search programs, so feel free to skip ahead if you are accustomed to using them.

Illustrations of web pages in this chapter are current as the book goes to press; however, the layout and design of websites or single web pages may be subject to change. Also, the illustrations are shown using Netscape version 4.7 as the browser. If you use a different browser software program, such as Microsoft Explorer, pages may appear in a slightly different format but all essential features will be the same.

Reference databases provide a relatively easy way to find studies of interest. Typically, each entry or **citation** for an article gives its title, author(s), and publication date, and the name of the journal in which it was published, including volume and/or issue and page numbers. A short descriptive summary or **abstract** of the article's main points is frequently included, although older references (those prior to 1975) may not have abstracts available, or may use the first paragraph of the article as the abstract.

The title, author, journal name, publication date, and other bibliographic information are called **fields**. You can use fields to narrow searches so that you are retrieving only citations that are relevant to your purpose; searches can sometimes turn up hundreds of articles. Limiting or refining the search in such a situation can save you a great deal of time. On the other hand, to get a comprehensive view you may want to combine results from several searches to include every aspect of a topic. Whether you limit or expand your search, the particular path you select is called a **search strategy**.

What If I Do Not Have a Computer?

Even if you don't have a computer at home, you may be able to use one at work or at school. Most institutions of higher learning provide students computer access. If you are unfamiliar with using a computer and browser software to access the World Wide Web, ask a reference librarian if instruction is available, or sign up for a short noncredit course at a local community college. Many public libraries offer Web access; if yours does not, ask the reference librarian for suggestions.

If you have the good fortune to live near a major research library, visit it and ask under what circumstances members of the public or health care providers who are not affiliated with the institution are allowed to use the library facilities. Some university and/or hospital-based medical libraries will allow local health care practitioners to use their services, with or without some restrictions, and these may offer access to more specialized databases, such as CINAHL, the Computerized Index to Nursing and Allied Health Literature, PsycINFO, the primary database for the behavioral sciences, or EMBASE, a European counterpart of MEDLINE. At the very least, you may be able to use a library computer to access PUBMED.

About PubMed

PubMed is the search service provided by the National Library of Medicine. It includes MEDLINE, the primary reference database maintained by the National Library of Medicine, along with PreMEDLINE, HealthStar, and other related health care databases. PubMed contains over eleven million bibliographic citations from more than 4,000 journals covering medical, nursing, dental, veterinary medicine, life sciences, and health care literature published in the United States and seventy other countries. Most entries are from English-language sources or have English abstracts available. The majority of citations are for articles published after 1965. PubMed is a comprehensive database covering conventional medicine, and in recent years many more articles on complementary and alternative therapies have been added as these have entered the mainstream of health care literature. PubMed is very current; citations are added daily.

Publishers who supply citations for articles and publisher sites that are linked to PubMed often allow the full text of selected articles to be viewed and printed out from your computer, although some charge fees of varying amounts. An asterisk at the link to the site indicates sites that charge for this service.

Using PubMed

Go to the PubMed website: http://www.ncbi.nih.nlm.gov/entrez. The page should look similar to Figure 2.1. Use the bookmark function on your browser to mark this address, so you won't have to retype it each time you visit the site. Look at the left margin of the screen under Entrez PubMed and click on Overview and FAQ (Frequently Asked Questions). Read these before proceeding further. You may want to print out the FAQ for easy reference.

If your web browser is not set to automatically accept cookies,* you will need to accept each one as it appears on the screen, or change your browser settings to accept them in order to access the widest array of PubMed features. If you would like to save your search strategy, click on Cubby

---

A cookie is a kind of tag or label that allows the website to store and keep track of information that you provide.

under PubMed Services and register now to use this service. Write down your password. A nice feature of Cubby is that it will automatically update your search for any new citations added to PubMed since your last search using that strategy.

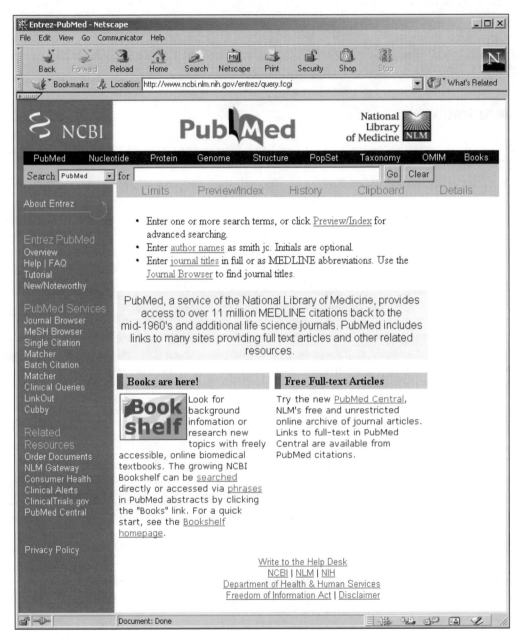

Figure 2.1 PubMed Home Page

Making Sense of Research

Performing a Search

Notice the query box and toolbar just under the headline at the top of the page as seen in Figure 2.2. To perform a simple search, just type the search term in the query box and click Go.

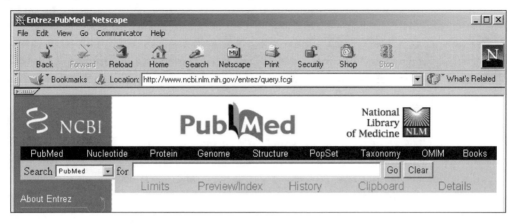

Figure 2.2   PubMed's Search Tools

The toolbar at the top of the page and sidebar to the left are available wherever you go in PubMed, so you can run a new search or click on other features at any point. You can use more than one term to search. For example, if you type in 'massage therapy,' PubMed will automatically combine the two terms, searching for 'massage' and 'therapy' in all the fields.

You can narrow your focus by clicking Limits in the Features bar directly below the query box. This allows you to restrict your search, say by the study participants' age or gender, or by the publication language, date or type. You can also limit your search to a particular subset of PubMed, such as AIDS-related citations, or citations in complementary medicine. Keeping the default 'all' setting allows you to search for the term in all of the citation fields. In addition, you can focus the search according to title, author, keyword, or textword.

Textword simply means any word found in the text or body of the abstract, and is the most general way to search for relevant articles. Using textword as a search field will usually retrieve the largest number of articles.

Keywords are specific words used to index an article and provide a controlled vocabulary that employs consistent descriptive language. In both PubMed and MEDLINE, the keywords are from MeSH, which stands for Medical Subject Headings. A list of MeSH with specific terms used to identify articles on alternative and complementary medicine can be found by clicking MeSh Browser from the left sidebar. If you are having trouble retrieving articles on a topic for which you know published research is available, check MeSH for keywords that might better describe your topic, or use textword to search for the term in the body of the abstract.

To preview the results of your search, click Preview. Preview allows you to see how many results you retrieved before the citations are displayed. If the number of results seems excessive you may want to refine your search using what are called **Boolean operators**. These are conjunctions such as *and*, *or*, and *not*. Boolean operators allow you to restrict your search in specific ways: *and* requires that all terms be present; *or* requires that at least one of the terms be present; *not* excludes citations with that particular term. An example of a search strategy using Boolean operators might look like this: massage AND cancer OR oncology NOT prostatic massage. This strategy would retrieve articles pertaining to both massage and cancer but not those concerning massage of the prostate gland, a procedure performed by physicians. Note that in PubMed you must type operators in all caps.

Clicking History allows you to see all your search strategies and results in one place, as illustrated in Figure 2.3. You have to run at least one search to access History. History lists and numbers your searches in the order in which you ran them, and displays the search number, the search terms used, and the number of citations retrieved. To view the citations retrieved, click the number of search results. This is the blue number on the far right of the page.* From either Preview or History, you can run new searches or combine results from previous searches. Be aware that in PubMed the search history is lost after one hour of inactivity.

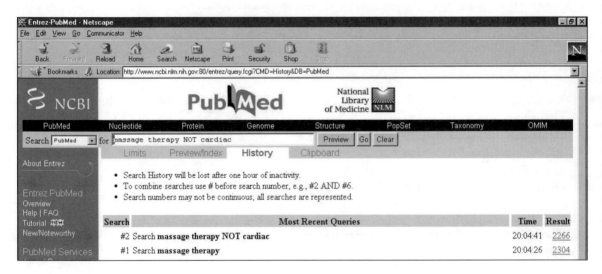

Figure 2.3   Viewing Your Search History

Clipboard is a feature that provides a place to collect selected citations from one or more searches. You can then print, save, or order citations. To add a citation to Clipboard, click the check box to its left and then click Add to Clipboard. After you have added an item to Clipboard, the search

---

* On the Web, text that is highlighted in blue will usually link you to another page or site.

record number color will turn green. As with History, citations in Clipboard are lost after one hour of inactivity.

Viewing Search Results

PubMed displays search results in batches, usually twenty to a page. Click Display, and from the Summary drop down menu select the Abstract format to view abstracts of the articles found in your search. Choose the MEDLINE format if you want to save citations to a bibliographic reference software program such as Reference Manager® or ProCite.® Choosing one of these two formats also allows you to use the Related Articles and Link Out functions. The page will show a group of citations listing the author, title, and journal information, organized by date with the most recent at the top. It will look similar to the page shown in Figure 2.4.

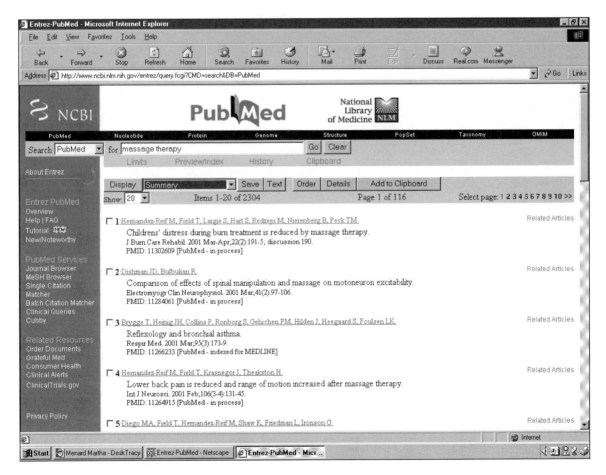

Figure 2.4   Viewing the List of Citations Found in a Search

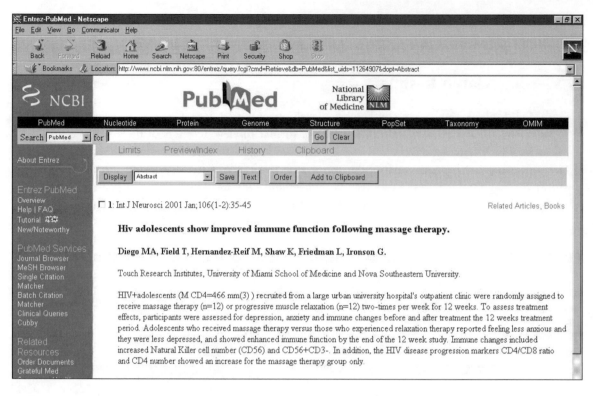

Figure 2.5   Viewing a Citation, Beginning with the Text of its Abstract

Click on the name of the author to view the complete citation with the abstract, as shown in Figure 2.5. You will notice to the right of the citation are links to Related Articles and LinkOut. If you find an article that is exactly what you are looking for, Related Articles allows you to quickly go to another similar article. LinkOut takes you to publishers' sites where you can view or print full text copies of selected articles or find other consumer health information. There may be a fee involved. A typical LinkOut screen is shown in Figure 2.6.

Use the Select Page feature (see Figure 2.4) to go to other pages containing more search results. When you want to keep search results, you can save the entire batch, which is the default setting, or you can use Add to Clipboard to save selected citations. From Clipboard you can also print out selected citations using the print function on your browser.

Saving Search Strategies

Use Cubby to save search strategies or view previously saved strategies. If you have not registered to use Cubby, go to the left sidebar and click Cubby, then click "I Want to Register for Cubby," and fill out the online form. Then log in to access Cubby. To save a search strategy, run or

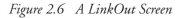

Back   Forward   Reload   Home   Search   Netscape   Print   Security   Shop   Stop

Bookmarks   Location: http://www.ncbi.nlm.nih.gov:80/entrez/query.fcgi?cmd=Retrieve&db=PubMed&list_uids=8707483&dopt=ExternalLink

NCBI

PubMed

National Library of Medicine NLM

| PubMed | Nucleotide | Protein | Genome | Structure | PopSet | Taxonomy | OMIM |

Search [PubMed ▾] for [   ] [Go] [Clear]

Limits   Preview/Index   History   Clipboard

About Entrez

Entrez PubMed
Overview
Help | FAQ
Tutorial
New/Noteworthy

PubMed Services
Journal Browser
MeSH Browser
Single Citation Matcher
Batch Citation Matcher
Clinical Queries
Cubby

Related Resources
Order Documents
Grateful Med

[Display] [LinkOut ▾] [Save] [Text] [Order] [Add to Clipboard]

• Links to full-text and resource information are supplied by LinkOut providers.
• Links with an asterisk (*) indicate the LinkOut provider requires a subscription, membership, or fee for access.

☐ 1: Ironson G, et al. Massage therapy is associated ...[PMID:8707483]   Related Articles

• OTHER:
  ■ Community of Science

[Display] [LinkOut ▾] [Save] [Text] [Order] [Add to Clipboard]

Figure 2.6   A LinkOut Screen

preview your search. Click Cubby from the sidebar. Edit the name of your search, using a phrase that will be meaningful to you later. Cubby will not accept numbers or dates as search names. Click on Store in Cubby to save.

Ordering Articles from PubMed

When you identify an article that meets your needs you often want to have a hard copy of it. If the journal is part of a university library's holdings, you may be able to make a copy of the article there. Some articles are also available on the Web and can be downloaded and printed directly from your computer. Some articles may be available from the publisher; use Link Out to determine which these are and to access them. If these options are not available, the National Library of Medicine (NLM) provides a document delivery service called Loansome Doc. For a small fee, you can arrange delivery with a regional medical library.

Using Loansome Doc for the first time is a two-step process, and it will take some time for you to register. First, from the PubMed homepage, click Order Documents from the left sidebar, then click Registration from the Loansome Doc Ordering System page. Click on the web address highlighted in blue to search for a participating library in your area, and check to see whether its services are available to the public or to unaffiliated health professionals.

Each library determines its own document delivery service policies and fees. Usually these are reasonable, especially if you register as a health professional. The library I use charges $6.00 per article and mails a copy within two days of receiving my request. Faxing is quicker, but most libraries charge substantially more for this service, and print quality is often poor.

Before you begin to use the Loansome Doc service to order hard copies of articles, you must sign an agreement with a participating library, who will then issue you the Library Identifier number used to register for Loansome Doc. This is the second step. After you have identified a suitable library close to you, click its address (it should be highlighted in blue) and see if its agreement form is available online. If it is, print it, fill it out, and fax or mail it back to the library. The library will then contact you, which may take some time, but once you have the Library Identifier number you can complete the Loansome Doc registration form shown in Figure 2.7. After you have registered and have a Library Identifier number, it is a simple process to order an article as you are searching PubMed by clicking Order at the bottom of the page.

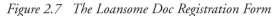

Figure 2.7   The Loansome Doc Registration Form

If you need more assistance or would rather speak directly to someone, in the United States call 1-800-338-7657 during normal business hours. In Canada, if your local health sciences library does not provide Loansome Doc services, you can set up an agreement with the Canada Institute for Scientific and Technical Information (CISTI), based in Ottawa, Ontario. From the LOANSOME DOC Registration page, select Canada from the drop down menu and go to the CISTI website to register. If you live outside North America, select Other Countries from the drop down menu.

Other PubMed Features

When you are viewing any of the PubMed pages illustrated in Figures 2.1 through 2.6, look at the bottom of the left sidebar under Related Resources. Clicking Consumer Health will take you to MEDLINE*plus*, where, in addition to searching MEDLINE, you can access articles on various health-related topics, find locations or credentials for doctors and hospitals, and link to other organizations. Another Related Resource, called Clinical Alerts, contains the results of recent clinical trials conducted through the National Institutes of Health (NIH). In addition, ClinicalTrials.gov is a website that provides consumer information about the clinical trial process and a list of clinical trials currently being conducted for patients who may wish to enroll.

What if I Need More Help Using PubMed?

Click on Help, and look through the menu to see if your question is listed there. You can also click on Write to Help Desk or send an email to pubmed@ncbi.nlm.nih.gov. Or you can call the NLM customer service desk at 1-888-346-3656, Monday through Friday from 8:30 a.m. to 8:45 p.m. and Saturday from 10:00 a.m. to 5:00 p.m. Eastern time.

Other Resources

Several medical journals publish online editions that allow access to selected articles at no charge as an incentive to visit their site and subscribe. Some of the better known journals include:

Alternative Therapies in Health and Medicine   http://www.alternative-therapies.com

The Journal of the American Medical Association   http://jama.ama-assn.org/issues

British Medical Journal   http://www.bmj.com

The Lancet   http://www.thelancet.com

The New England Journal of Medicine   http://www.nejm.org

The Townsend Letter for Doctors and Patients   http://www.tldp.com

The Physician and Sportsmedicine   http://www.physsportsmed.com   (access back issues search)

Direct access to current issues of several hundred full-text medical journals can be found at FreeMedicalJournals.com. Journals are arranged in alphabetical order and by specialty. Most of the journals listed here are conventional but *Alternative Medicine Review* is available. The address is http://www.freemedicaljournals.com.

Another website, *Alternative Health News Online*, provides current information related to complementary therapies, including recent research studies of interest to complementary practitioners, and links to several of the websites listed above. The address is http://www.altmedicine.com. A number of other sites offer access to lesser known sources of CAM journal articles, some of which can accommodate individual searches but may charge a fee.

For a list of additional databases that can be searched, visit the website of the Rosenthal Center for Complementary and Alternative Medicine at Columbia University, one of ten NCCAM-funded centers in the United States. The address is http://cpmcnet.columbia.edu/dept/rosenthal. From the welcome page, click CAM Research and Information Resources, then click Directory of Databases. Many of the databases listed, such as EMBASE, are not publicly accessible. However, a medical reference librarian can conduct a search for you for a fee.

While you are scrolling down the Directory page, notice in particular the CISCOM database. CISCOM stands for Centralised Information Service for Complementary Medicine. It is maintained by the Research Council for Complementary Medicine (RCCM) in London, England. It includes citations from European databases and other sources not found in MEDLINE. The RCCM will perform customized searches for a fee. Or, using the RCCM home page you can search selected citations from CISCOM and download prepackaged lists of citations organized by therapeutic modality, including acupuncture, aromatherapy, chiropractic, healing, homeopathy, hypnotherapy, and manipulation. There is also an extensive overview of massage therapy and a list of citations about research on touch. Each list contains approximately 200 citations; many but not all contain abstracts as well. Click CISCOM from the Rosenthal Center page, or visit the RCCM home page at http://www.rccm.org.uk.

Other specific therapies sources include the Consortium for Chiropractic Research, the Society for Acupuncture Research, and the American Massage Therapy Association Foundation. Like the Rosenthal Center, the Consortial Center for Chiropractic Research is funded by NCCAM. The web address is http://www.c3r.org/home. A list of all projects currently sponsored by the Center is posted there. Additional web pages listing citations related to chiropractic research can be found at http://www.chiroweb.com/archives/10/04/05.html and at http://www.chiro.org. The website of the International Chiropractic Online Network, http://www.chiropage.com, contains links to a number of articles on chiropractic research and several online journals.

The Society for Acupuncture Research (SAR) is based in Bethesda, Maryland, and sponsors an annual research conference. SAR has a list of seventy clinical trials of acupuncture outcomes available for a fee, however, these are studies with positive outcomes only. Contact SAR at their website http://www.acupunctureresearch.org.

The American Massage Therapy Association Foundation has a comprehensive database of research across a variety of touch-based therapies. You can visit the Foundation's website at http://www.amtafoundation.org. From the sidebar on the top, click Research Database.

Finally, the NIH maintains a database of federally funded research projects including those currently in progress, called the Computer Retrieval of Information on Scientific Projects, or CRISP. CRISP covers a wide spectrum of scientific research funded by a variety of federal agencies, and is not limited to CAM research. This database can be used to identify specific projects or investigators, and to take note of emerging trends and research methods. To search CRISP, visit its website at http://crisp.cit.nih.gov. You can search for either current or past projects by clicking the appropriate query form on the left side of the page.

The Web offers a multitude of resources for anyone interested in learning more about finding and understanding health care research. The information covered here is a brief introduction that can help you get started. Have fun exploring.

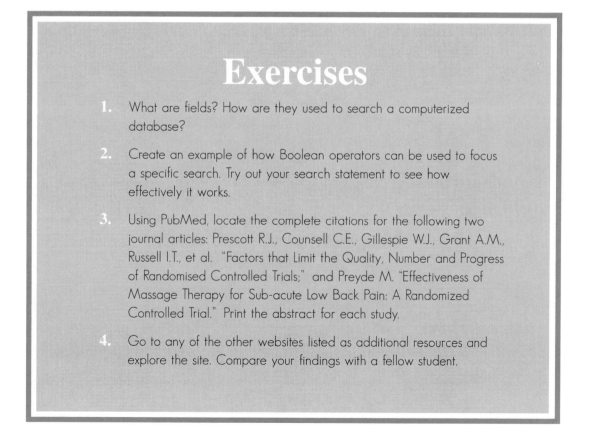

Exercises

1. What are fields? How are they used to search a computerized database?

2. Create an example of how Boolean operators can be used to focus a specific search. Try out your search statement to see how effectively it works.

3. Using PubMed, locate the complete citations for the following two journal articles: Prescott R.J., Counsell C.E., Gillespie W.J., Grant A.M., Russell I.T., et al. "Factors that Limit the Quality, Number and Progress of Randomised Controlled Trials;" and Preyde M. "Effectiveness of Massage Therapy for Sub-acute Low Back Pain: A Randomized Controlled Trial." Print the abstract for each study.

4. Go to any of the other websites listed as additional resources and explore the site. Compare your findings with a fellow student.

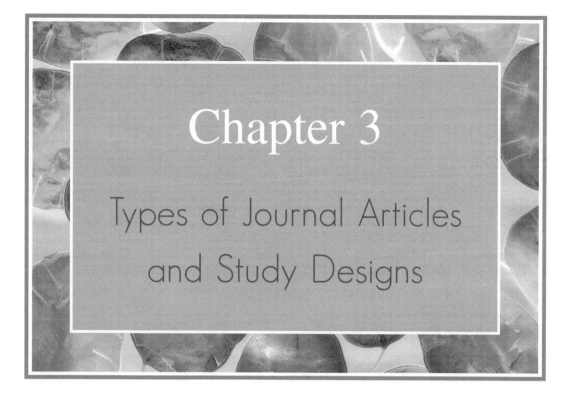

Chapter 3

Types of Journal Articles and Study Designs

Observation is a critical and purposive process; there is a scientific reason for making one observation rather than another . . . Experimentation, too, is a critical process, one that discriminates between possibilities and gives direction to further thought.

P. B. Medawar

Learning Objectives

- Describe three general types of articles found in peer reviewed journals.

- Identify five types of clinical research designs.

- Explain the strengths and weaknesses of these designs in providing evidence of cause and effect.

When we think of health care research and the journals in which such research is published, we usually think first of reports of experimental studies. In this chapter and the next, we will look at the structure of these studies and other types of clinical research in more detail. We will also consider the relative strengths of each type of study design in judging whether cause and effect relationships exist among the study variables. Recognizing and understanding study design types alerts you to the potential strengths and weaknesses you are likely to encounter as you read and evaluate a given study.

A major consideration when evaluating a study is to what extent the research design and methods used are a good fit with the question. The research question may be clearly articulated and highly significant, but if the design and/or methods are poorly suited to answer it, the findings may be inconclusive, misleading, or not interpretable. Particularly in massage therapy research, the appropriateness of the massage protocol to the question should be thoughtfully examined.

Reports of experimental studies are not the only published writings you will come across as you read. Before we begin our focus on clinically related research, we will consider other types of articles that are found in peer-reviewed journals. Two of these that are especially useful to practitioners and other research consumers are **letters to the editor** and **literature reviews.**

Letters to the Editor

Letters to the editor are often profitable to read. They can provide commentary on previous articles, share clinical situations that the author has encountered, or contribute new data in the form of brief reports or observations. Because these are not peer-reviewed, one should be cautious about giving one opinion too much weight. Letters that offer critiques of the methods used in previously published articles can be especially helpful. Such critiques can bring to our attention issues that we had not previously considered. Depending on the persuasiveness of the author's argument, a letter can change our opinion. Some letters will also cite other articles to back up the author's arguments, and following up on these references can add to the reader's understanding of the issues. References listed in letters can sometimes provide a source of more obscure or hard to find citations from other published studies.

Literature Reviews

Literature reviews can be an invaluable resource. They provide an overview of a particular research question and identify key studies in that area. Although review articles will show up in a general search, they can also be searched for specifically by using "review" or "meta-analysis" as key words. Literature reviews fall into three categories:

- the narrative review or survey of the literature
- the meta-analysis
- a more specialized type of meta-analysis, the systematic review

Bibliographies of review articles are also a good source of related studies. For someone looking for a synopsis of current thinking on a research question, a recent literature review is an excellent place to start. It can tell you, among other things, which articles are worth your time reading completely.

• Narrative Reviews

The narrative review examines a group of studies in a particular subject area and, as all literature reviews do, attempts to come to some conclusion based on a synthesis of the group as a whole. The author determines which studies are selected to form the group, and this feature can be both a strength and a weakness. The primary strength of the narrative review is that the author can discuss the methods and conclusions of important studies in detail, and give an opinion about their relative merits. A major weakness of narrative reviews is the risk associated with author selection; in some cases, the author may be unaware of or unable to access all the relevant studies. Poorer quality studies may be included and treated as equal to better quality studies. The author may also choose to ignore studies with outcomes that are not consistent with the hypothesis presented, although this practice is not considered acceptable and is (one hopes) not common.

There are several examples of narrative reviews that are pertinent to the field of massage therapy. A well known and excellent example is the review of research on touch compiled by anthropologist Ashley Montague in his book *Touching*.[1] Montague integrates research from several areas and makes a compelling case for his argument that touch is a biological necessity for human survival and optimal well-being.

A narrative review that attempts to document the psychological and physiological effects of massage was done by Tiffany Field.[2] This review is noteworthy for its interesting discussion of possible mechanisms that might explain the effects in the studies listed. However, a weakness of the review is that it does not consider studies that produced negative results, and few studies other than those conducted by the Touch Research Institute are included.

Another example is a review written by a practitioner, Phyllis Keenan, that offers a somewhat more balanced approach. It is a compilation of studies on the benefits of massage and use of a doula during labor and birth.[3] This review presents both positive and negative study results, for instance noting that while perineal massage performed during pregnancy reduces the rates of tearing and cesarean section, perineal massage performed during labor shows no benefit.

• Meta-analyses

The meta-analysis, developed as a way to improve upon the weaknesses of the narrative review, has increasingly become a more popular form of literature review. Meta-analysis is possible as a result of the development of computerized databases which make locating studies much easier, and is more necessary than ever before in health care due to the expanding volume of research studies. In a meta-analysis studies on a particular question are grouped according to pre-established criteria; a literature search using one or more major databases is conducted to find all the articles that meet those criteria. This practice is analogous to specifying eligibility criteria for clinical study participants prior to their recruitment into the study. Defining the criteria for inclusion in advance reduces the potential for selection bias on the part of the investigator.

Results of the studies that meet the criteria are then pooled, that is, combined so that the statistical power of the grouped studies is much greater than each single study alone. Meta-analysis is often used to estimate the size of a treatment effect or to settle a question when there are several contradictory or inconclusive studies with small numbers of participants. An important consideration in evaluating a meta-analysis is whether the studies that have been pooled are similar enough in terms of their hypotheses tested and outcomes measured. One criticism of this method is that while it can be an improvement over the more subjective narrative review, meta-analysis can sometimes pool such disparate studies that in effect the authors are combining apples and oranges. If the research question is about fruit salad, so to speak, there is no problem. If not, the results can be misleading. This is a particular risk in fields like massage therapy where the interventions used can vary so widely.

Another concern with meta-analysis is that **publication bias** has the potential to skew the results. Publication bias refers to the tendency for journals to reject studies with negative or inconclusive results and to be more likely to publish those with positive results. Because it is therefore probable that studies with negative findings are less likely to be included in any subsequent analysis, their absence can prejudice the results, for example, by making an intervention appear more effective than it really is.

•   Systematic Reviews

The systematic review is a more refined version of the meta-analysis. It attempts to compensate for publication bias by making additional efforts, such as locating dissertations, hand searching journals that are not indexed in computerized databases, and personally communicating with authors of unpublished studies to identify every relevant study on a given research question. These are then usually weighted in terms of the strength and quality of the evidence presented. For example, a study employing random assignment of participants to an intervention or a control group would be weighted more heavily than one without these design features. Standardized methods for weighting studies based on internal validity and for statistical analysis are used.

•   *The Cochrane Collaboration*

Systematic reviews have been popularized by the Cochrane Collaboration, a voluntary group of health care providers, consumers, and scientists named for the late British physician and epidemiologist Archie Cochrane. Dr. Cochrane was a pioneer of the evidence-based medicine movement who strongly believed in the use of systematic reviews in shifting medical care towards practice based on research evidence. For more information on the Cochrane Collaboration, including abstracts of systematic reviews, visit their website: http://www.cochrane.org.

Since its inception in 1993, the Cochrane Collaboration has completed over 600 reviews, and another 600 are planned. A working group interested in complementary medicine has been formed and several systematic reviews have been conducted. An early review, on the use of massage for premature infants, was updated in October 1999.[4] An abstract of this study can be viewed at the Cochrane website. From the home page, click "Abstracts of Cochrane Reviews," then click "Cochrane Neonatal Group." Scroll down the list of studies to the title "Massage for Promoting Growth and Development of Preterm and/or Low Birth-weight Infants."

Another Cochrane review has been conducted on the use of massage for low back pain.[5] This study uses a slightly different method of systematic review called *best evidence synthesis*.[6] Best evidence synthesis developed as a way to combine the quantitative features of meta-analysis with the advantages of the qualitative narrative review, and is used when the studies that are located turn out to be too different from one another or lack sufficient data to be pooled as is done in a traditional meta-analysis. Instead, reviewers evaluate the selected studies by carefully considering the evidence presented in each one, and then draw an overall conclusion about where the weight of the evidence lies. Systematic reviews can be expected to continue to gain popularity as a way to synthesize a large quantity of research on disputed questions and render verdicts.

Guidelines for Evaluating Literature Reviews

Evaluating literature reviews in depth is a detailed and technically challenging subject, with methods that continue to be refined. However, several general guidelines can be applied to assess the quality of a review:[7]

1. The research question addressed by the review should be specific and clearly defined.

2. The methods used to locate studies should be described, along with the criteria for inclusion or exclusion of studies from the review.

3. If studies are ranked or weighted, the internal validity of the studies included should be assessed according to objective and reproducible methods, and the weighting methods should be described.

4. If a meta-analysis was performed, the pooled data should be combined appropriately (apples with apples). A table that lists the individual studies with brief summaries describing the participants, methods, and results of each study helps the reader to judge similarities.

5. Just as in any research study, the reviewers' conclusions should be supported by the data presented.

Clinically Related Health Care Research

Epidemiologists are scientists who study the causes of disease. Although the principles of research design are the same in every discipline, epidemiology as a field has developed specialized methods to determine whether a relationship exists between a particular cause and a disease, and if so, to assess the strength of that relationship. The terms that epidemiologists prefer to use, rather than cause and disease, are **exposure** and **outcome**. An exposure can refer to a factor such as smoking that predisposes someone to develop an outcome like heart disease or cancer, or it can refer to a protective factor such as exercise that reduces the risk of developing the condition. An outcome can refer to development of a disease or to any clinical endpoint of interest such as heart rate, urinary cortisol level, or quality of life. Given its role in preventing and controlling the spread of infectious disease, it is understandable that epidemiological research places a major emphasis on determining whether a cause and effect relationship exists between an exposure and an outcome.

Classification of Studies

Epidemiologists have developed several ways of classifying the various types of studies and the terminology used to describe them. No matter what methods or design strategies are used to answer a research question, the goal of almost all clinically related research is to describe or explain events. As a result, studies can be grouped into two broad categories: **descriptive** and **explanatory**.

Descriptive studies do just that: they provide a record or description of events or activities. Explanatory studies seek to elucidate connections between events or variables and can be further divided into **observational** and **experimental** studies. In an observational study, the researcher attempts to explain a connection between naturally occurring events, such as exposure to one or more risk factors or predictors and the subsequent development of an outcome, without manipulating those events. In an experimental study, the researcher manipulates events, for example by giving a treatment and then assessing its effects. Figure 3.1 illustrates these different types of studies. Explanations and examples of the various kinds of descriptive, observational, and experimental studies follow.

Descriptive Studies

Descriptive studies are considered weaker evidence of a cause and effect relationship largely because they lack a control or comparison group, a necessary feature. However, they can suggest further hypotheses to be tested, provide detailed information to help refine the design of an explanatory study, and, in combination with consistent results from observational or experimental studies, can add to the cumulative weight of evidence on a given question.

DESCRIPTIVE

Documents and communicates
clinician experiences, thoughts,
or observations

|

Used to form hypotheses

|

Examples:

Case Study
*Adverse response
to treatment*

•

Case Series
*Shiatsu used to treat
30 clients with
migraine headaches*

•

**Correlational
Study**
*Rates of population
growth and
contraceptive sales*

•

**Qualitative
Study**
*Patients' experience
of the therapeutic
relationship*

EXPLANATORY

Examines causes, etiology,
or treatment efficacy by
comparing groups

|

Used to test hypotheses

EXPERIMENTAL

Evaluates
efficacy

|

Investigator controls

|

Examples:

**Before & After
Treatment**
*Effect of a
single massage
on pain*

•

Clinical Trial
*P6 point
stimulation for
morning sickness*

OBSERVATIONAL

Seeks causes,
factors, predictors

|

Investigator observes

|

Examples:

**Cross-sectional
Study**
*Survey of patients
seeking treatment
at a school clinic*

•

**Case-control
Study**
*Exercise patterns
in type 2 diabetics
vs. non-diabetics*

•

Cohort Study
*Development of
repetitive use injuries
in massage therapists*

Figure 3.1 Types of Study Designs

•   Case Studies

The simplest form of descriptive study is the case study or report, which describes the events related to the care of a single patient. The case study usually features some unusual aspect of the health history, assessment, or effect of treatment, although it will occasionally be used to present a typical or textbook example of a case and its successful resolution, or to report an innovation in assessment or treatment. Although the case study does not provide the same weight of evidence as a randomized controlled trial, it is valuable as a basis for developing new hypotheses. Case studies may also be used to report adverse responses to treatment or to document unusual events, thus alerting other practitioners. What separates the case study from an anecdote is a compelling rationale for its presentation, thorough description, relevant detail, and a discussion of contradictory evidence or observations along with directions for future investigations or for managing similar cases.

•   Case Series

Case series take the case study method a step further by combining individual case studies of similar patients; they are often the first indication of a new disease or an adverse effect resulting from a new medication or procedure. A good example is the July 1981 report from the Centers for Disease Control[8] describing an unusual number of cases of Kaposi's sarcoma among young, previously healthy gay men at a time when this form of cancer was typically seen in the elderly. This case series was one of several reports that heralded the beginning of the AIDS epidemic. Case studies and case series raise potential research questions but alone cannot provide evidence of a *valid* association, that is, whether there is a true causal relationship between the factors or exposures observed and the later development of an outcome or disease.

> **QUESTIONS FOR EVALUATING CASE STUDIES AND CASE SERIES**
>
> 1. Is the subject interesting or useful to your practice?
> 2. Is there a clear statement of the clinical importance of the case? Are references provided?
> 3. Is all relevant patient data reported in sufficient detail?
> 4. Is the treatment provided described adequately?
> 5. Are other plausible explanations considered?
> 6. Are the strengths and weaknesses, implications, and relevance of this case to other similar cases discussed?
> 7. Are directions for future studies in this area or management of similar cases discussed?

•   Correlational Studies

The correlational study, or population survey, uses aggregated group data that already exists about large populations rather than having to be collected directly from individuals by the investigator. These studies are very useful as a quick way to see whether an association between an exposure and outcome exists. For example, a well-known correlational study first described patterns of death from coronary heart disease in 1960 in relationship to per capita cigarette sales across the United States.[9] As sales of cigarettes (exposure) increased during that time, so did death rates (outcome). Correlational studies are often a next step in testing a new hypothesis because they are relatively low cost, simple, and quick to conduct using data available from public agencies.

A correlational study describes or demonstrates a statistical association between an exposure and an outcome, but does not explain it. One cannot assume from correlation alone that a causal relationship exists between the exposure and the outcome. Other factors may be involved. For example, as the number of churches in a city increases, so does the number of alcoholics.* It would be a mistake to conclude on this evidence alone that going to church therefore causes alcoholism. Numbers of churches and alcoholics are both functions of population increase; if you compare a small city with a large one, you will find that the large city has more churches and more alcoholics because it has more people. It is also not clear which came first, more churches or more alcoholics. Thus, correlation alone does not indicate causation. Such a spurious relationship between an exposure and an outcome due to the effects of a related factor is another example of confounding. Confounding as an alternative explanation needs to be considered by the reader in almost all types of clinical studies, including experimental ones.

Conversely, lack of correlation does not guarantee that a causal relationship does not exist. Rather than jumping to conclusions about causation, the key issue in evaluating a correlational study is the strength of the evidence presented in demonstrating that an association exists.

•   Qualitative Studies

Although they are not usually considered in epidemiology texts, qualitative studies deserve a special mention as another type of descriptive study. As discussed in Chapter 1, qualitative methods are preferred when investigating topics about which little is known. In recent years, more qualitative studies are being performed within health care research, particularly in the field of nursing. They are often utilized as a way to gain insight into the experiences, choices, and behaviors of patients and providers.[10] Such research is valuable in its own right as a part of evidence-based health care, and also provides important information that can be used to design better quantitative studies. Because of the complex nature of many CAM therapies and the importance of the therapeutic relationship between client and practitioner, the field can benefit greatly from more qualitative research. We will explore qualitative methodology and evaluation in more depth in Chapter 7.

I am indebted to UVA statistics professor Don Ball for this example.

Explanatory Studies

Explanatory studies seek to test hypotheses, clarify or establish cause-and-effect relationships, and ideally to provide evidence about questions such as disease prevalence and treatment efficacy. As was mentioned earlier, this broad category of studies is divided into observational and experimental subgroups.

• Observational Studies

Observational studies attempt to explain the relationship between exposure and outcome by observing the natural course of events, collecting information about the people or events involved, and then sorting them into groups based on that data. By comparing the groups, an investigator hopes to draw conclusions about the relationship between exposure and outcome. An example of this kind of study would be one that shows a correlation between levels of education in the general population and the degree to which people use complementary therapies. Observational studies are sometimes referred to as **analytical studies**. Types of observational studies include:

- cross-sectional studies

- case-control studies

- cohort studies

• *Cross-sectional Studies*

One way to classify the different kinds of observational studies is based on the time at which exposures and outcomes are measured. In a cross-sectional study, data regarding the exposure and outcome are simultaneously collected across a population at a specific point in time, then sorted and compared. This design provides a snapshot of a particular situation, which can be a specific moment or period of time, or some significant marker that can vary from person to person. Examples would be admission to a professional training program or the birth of a first child. Surveys are a familiar example of the cross-sectional study. We will look more closely at a model survey in the next chapter.

Cross-sectional studies are frequently used to identify predictive or causal factors or to determine the prevalence* of a problem or a specific occurrence. For example, in a prevalence study researchers might catalog the kinds of health problems reported among clients who are seeking treatment at a student clinic in an acupuncture school. Demographic data,* together with

---

* Prevalence is defined as the number of cases of existing disease or outcome per population at risk; basically, how common is it at this point in time?
* Includes characteristics such as age, sex, educational level, regional location, ethnicity, annual income, socio-economic status, or others that can be used to describe or classify groups.

different types of health problems occurring in the group, might then be analyzed to see who is using the clinic, and what health problems are common among them. Some types of people might report certain conditions more frequently; for example, there may be a high number of older men with osteoarthritis, or of young women and infants with HIV. Knowing the demographics of clinic users and the conditions seen more frequently in the clinic would be helpful for educators planning coursework to prepare students to work in the clinic. Cross-sectional studies can also be used to predict risk factors linked to an outcome. Early studies of the AIDS epidemic showed that the disease was more prevalent among gay men as well as individuals who had received blood transfusions as compared to others without these exposures.

Cross-sectional studies are generally used in the early stages of an investigation to 'map out the territory.' They provide a great deal of descriptive information and can often be conducted quickly and cheaply by using existing data. However, there is a significant problem with this design. Because exposure and outcome are assessed at the same time, it may be impossible to determine which came first. If people with osteoarthritis tend to be overweight, is it because their joint problems prevented them from getting enough exercise to keep their weight down? Or did the excess weight increase the amount of wear and tear on their joints in the first place?

• *Case-control Studies*

In the case-control design, the second type of observational study, both the outcome and exposure have already occurred, and selection is made based on whether individuals do or do not have the outcome of interest. Investigators identify a group with a disease (cases) and then compare them to another group without the disease (controls). Case-control studies are sometimes referred to as **retrospective studies.** Predictive factors are analyzed by looking backwards in time and examining the kinds and degrees of exposures between the two groups. This type of study has become more widespread during the past fifty years as epidemiology has focused more on the risk factors associated with chronic illnesses.

This design has the advantage of allowing the researcher to explore many different exposures along with the possibility of interrelationships among them. The disadvantage is that because both the exposure and the outcome have already happened by the time participants are selected for the study, two potential sources of bias are introduced. Bias can enter either from the way in which cases and controls are defined and selected, or from a lack of accuracy or completeness in the data collected regarding the exposure. To avoid bias, the disease or outcome should be clearly defined and diagnostic criteria specified prior to the selection of individual cases and controls; cases and controls must truly be comparable to each other in everything except their exposure. Patients documented as having a general reproductive cancer diagnosis, for example, may have different specific types of uterine and ovarian cancer, each with different risk factors or causes. In another example, patients selected from a tertiary care hospital that provides more specialized care may differ in significant ways from patients seen in a community based hospital; patients in the former are more likely to be more seriously ill, and conditions that are less frequent in a general hospital population may appear more often.

It is more difficult to avoid bias in collecting data from participants regarding amount or degree of exposure. Participants may not remember events accurately or may be reluctant to disclose information about their habits, a phenomenon sometimes referred to as **recall bias**. A case-control study setting out to examine the role of diet in the development of cancer might depend upon participants remembering how often they ate red meat historically or being willing to reveal the quantity of alcohol they consumed daily. Also, the same 'chicken-or-egg' problem regarding the temporal relationship of exposure to outcome seen in the cross-sectional study can occur with the case-control design. It may not always be clear whether the exposure precedes the outcome or is a consequence of the outcome.

For the reader evaluating a case-control study, it is important to notice whether the authors have acknowledged these potential sources of bias. A well-designed study will discuss and/or estimate the role of any possible sources of bias that cannot be eliminated by the study's design.

- *Cohort Studies*

In the third type of observational study, the cohort study, the outcome has not yet occurred. A group or cohort is defined based on the presence or absence of their exposure to a risk factor, and the members of the group are followed over a span of time to see which ones develop the outcome. For this reason, cohort studies are sometimes called **longitudinal**, **follow-up**, or **prospective studies**.

Cohort studies avoid the problems of selection and recall bias associated with case-control studies and demonstrate stronger evidence that a cause and effect relationship exists than either cross-sectional or case-control designs. However, mortality (attrition of participants) is a major issue with cohort studies because studies using this design may follow participants for months, years, or even decades. Associated with this problem is the fact that people do sometimes change their habits or lifestyle; they take up exercise, stop drinking coffee, or get a new and more stressful job. Well-designed cohort studies periodically contact participants to appraise such changes.

A good example of an ongoing cohort study is the Nurses' Health Study, which enrolled 120,000 married female registered nurses in the United States after the initial surveys were mailed out during the mid 1970s. A baseline questionnaire was used to collect information regarding medical history along with demographic, reproductive, and lifestyle variables. Every two years since, participants have provided follow-up information on the baseline variables, on new variables that have been added, and on the development of outcomes. Comparing women who have been exposed to risk factors such as hormone use or a family history of disease with those who have not has provided considerable data about relationship of such factors to the subsequent development of cardiovascular disease and cancer. This study, among other epidemiological studies, raised serious questions regarding the risks and benefits of hormone replacement therapy, and led to the Women's Health Initiative Randomized Control Trial which showed an association between HRT and breast cancer risk.

Observational study designs provide stronger evidence of a valid association between exposure and outcome than do descriptive studies. Both cross-sectional and case-control designs can be problematic in terms of determining whether the exposure precedes the outcome. Cohort designs, which provide the strongest evidence, avoid this problem but pose their own challenges, and are expensive as well as time-consuming to conduct.

•   **Experimental Studies**

There are several key differences between experimental studies and other kinds of research studies:

1. A primary difference between an experimental study and an observational or descriptive study is the active intervention of the researcher. He or she assigns the exposure, for example a treatment of some kind, to the participants.

2. Ethical considerations are a primary concern. Investigators are not allowed to offer an intervention that appears to be harmful to participants or to withhold one that appears beneficial; there must be sufficient doubt in either direction to justify the experiment.

3. Participants in clinical studies must provide informed consent. The investigator is required to explain in understandable language the procedures and treatments to be performed on the individual should he or she choose to participate in the study, as well as the potential risks and benefits of the intervention, so that the individual can make an informed decision.

We will consider two kinds of experimental studies: the **before-and-after treatment design** and the **clinical trial**.

•   *Before-and-After Treatment Studies*

The before-and-after treatment design is frequently used by complementary practitioners conducting research in their own practices. A former director of the NCCAM, Wayne Jonas, has advocated this design as a useful and practical way to measure the effectiveness of complementary and alternative therapies. Basically, the before-and-after treatment design can be considered as a kind of case series. The practitioner defines a hypothesis, specifies eligibility criteria and methods to be used, collects pertinent baseline data, provides the treatment, and measures the outcome for a series of patients. An example of this design is an ongoing study at Centennial College in

Ontario, based on a pilot study by the author, examining the impact of massage therapy on pain sensation and unpleasantness among clients seen in their student clinic.

The primary weakness of the before-and-after treatment design is that it lacks a control group for comparison purposes and, according to Schneider and Jonas,[11] has the potential to overestimate the true size of the treatment effect by up to 40 percent. In addition, if the practitioner who provides the treatment also collects subjective data directly, there is the possibility that his or her patients may tend to report what they think the practitioner wants to hear. Despite these limitations, when done well the before-and-after treatment remains a useful type of design that can contribute valuable information towards more rigorous studies.

> **QUESTIONS FOR EVALUATING BEFORE AND AFTER STUDIES**
>
> 1. *Is the hypothesis clearly defined?*
> 2. *Was the analysis planned in advance?*
> 3. *How and when was data collected?*
> 4. *How were outcomes measured?*
> 5. *Are arguments for generalizability of results plausible?*

When evaluating before-and-after studies, notice whether the hypothesis is simply and clearly defined. As with any study, a vague research question will not produce useful information. Is it clear that the analysis was planned before the data was collected? Choosing the method of analysis after the data has been collected leaves open the possibility that the analysis was either an afterthought or tailored to produce the desired results, rather than having been planned as the most appropriate method for the study in advance. To minimize bias, careful measurement of baseline data and outcomes is especially important, as well as the issue of who performed the data collection. Consider whether any arguments presented for generalizing the results beyond the study group are reasonable. The use of a control group, if possible, greatly increases the strength of this design.

• *Clinical Trials*

The clinical trial, sometimes called an **intervention study**, a **randomized trial**, or a **randomized controlled trial (RCT)**, provides the most direct evidence of a cause and effect relationship between an exposure and an outcome. It is considered the gold standard of health care research design. What makes this design so powerful is the random assignment or allocation of treatment to participants. As discussed in Chapter 1, when properly implemented with sufficient numbers of participants, random assignment controls not only for known factors that could influence the outcome but also for those not anticipated at the outset, a boon to the clinical researcher who often cannot fully control the research setting. Incorporation of features such as blinding or using a placebo control increases the strength of the design.

Characteristics of Clinical Trials

There are several important questions to bear in mind when evaluating a clinical trial:

1. How is the study population defined: what are the criteria for entry into or exclusion from the study?

2. How were participants assigned to group(s)?

3. How well were treatment and data collection protocols described and adhered to?

4. How is the problem of attrition handled?

• The Study Population

The term 'population' can have several different meanings in health care literature. There is the reference population, which is the larger group to which the study findings can (hopefully) be generalized; the experimental population, which is the group of possible study participants, including those who decide not to participate; and the study population itself, the actual group of participants who are both eligible and willing to take part in the study. It is important to keep in mind that the study population is a small subset of the total experimental population, and its members are likely to be different from eligible candidates not willing to participate in the study.*

• *Sampling*

Because it is generally impossible to collect data from the total experimental population, researchers must select a smaller portion or **sample** of the total population to represent it. This is known as sampling, and a familiar example of the importance of sampling can be seen in opinion surveys. The key issue in sampling is that the study population should be representative of the total population, and there are a number of ways to accomplish this goal. Random or probability sampling means that every member of the total population has an equal chance of being included, and this is the best way to ensure that the results of the study reflect the total population. In national opinion surveys this goal is feasible. Much is known about the demographics of the total population of most countries, and it is relatively easy for a researcher to randomly select an equivalent percentage of the sample for each demographic group. In this way, a small sample of one to two thousand people can accurately represent the opinions of an entire country, because the proportions of the sample are equal to the composition of the total population. In clinical research, however, it is much harder and often impossible to have true random sampling.

---

* *Researchers across many different fields have found that people who volunteer to be part of a study are more likely to be female, older, better educated, and have higher socioeconomic status compared to those who choose not to volunteer.*

The reader will therefore have to determine through a close reading of the description of the methods used in the study just how representative the study group is of the reference population and to what extent the results can be generalized. The example of drawing patients from a tertiary care hospital compared to a community-based hospital again applies. Baseline demographic information on patients who are eligible but unwilling to participate is also helpful in making this decision.

- *Eligibility Criteria*

Authors may not define their eligibility criteria clearly using objective standards, thus introducing confusion and possible bias because participants have not been classified accurately. Criteria should also be based on acceptable definitions of the disease or condition being studied, and any techniques or measures used to make a diagnosis or assessment should be reasonably available to other comparable practitioners. As a hypothetical example, let us say that a study evaluating the effectiveness of massage therapy for runners classified participants based on the number of fast twitch fibers relative to slow twitch fibers in the quadriceps, as measured by a biopsy. Positive results were found only for those runners with a high number of fast twitch fibers. The inability of most massage therapists to perform muscle biopsies in their workplaces would severely limit the practical application of the results, as well as the reproducibility of the study.

• **Allocation of Participants**

Selection and allocation of participants to groups within the study is another issue to be considered when evaluating a clinical trial. Participants in the control or comparison group should as a matter of course be drawn from the same population as those who receive the intervention. Each group needs to be comparable in terms of risk factors and circumstances that might affect the outcome under study.

- *Random Assignment*

When random assignment has been used, it is important for the reader to determine exactly how it was carried out. It is not random assignment to assign study participants based on odd or even days of the week, on the flip of a coin, or on the convenience of their being in the right place at the right time. The crucial issue is whether all participants have an equal chance of being assigned to any of the study groups. Preferably, this has been achieved through the use of a randomly generated table of numbers. Patients in a study are generally given an ID number. An existing number such as their SSN or SIN may be used, or one is arbitrarily assigned. These numbers are matched to the table of random numbers to determine group assignment.

Only when random assignment is properly carried out can selection bias that might create differences between the groups be avoided. Prudent investigators check the data on relevant group

Making Sense of Research

characteristics to verify that randomization was successfully applied and balance among the groups was accomplished. Typically, this is one of the first tables of results presented in a published study, and it usually contains demographic data across all groups. If there are imbalances among groups with respect to known confounding variables after randomization, this type of imbalance can be compensated for during the statistical analysis of the study data.*

• Adherence to Protocols

Compliance refers to how faithfully a study's participants adhere to the requirements the study asks of them. Lack of compliance is a potential source of bias when treatments or their measurements are difficult, demanding, or unpleasant for participants. For example, they may fail to follow procedures because the medicine has disagreeable side effects or because keeping the daily food diary is too much trouble. A treatment may appear ineffective because the participants did not receive it as defined in the study protocol or because the measurement of outcome data is incomplete. As discussed in Chapter 1, unbeknownst to the investigator participants may seek out additional treatments or substitute other treatments as **co-interventions**. A co-intervention can be blatant, as in the use of herbal supplements that may interact with the medication being studied, or it may be something as subtle as extra attention from an assistant collecting the data. Distributed unevenly among groups as they tend to be, co-interventions can result in significant bias.

A related issue that poses obvious risks of introducing bias is how systematically investigators carried out the study procedures or protocol. The discussion of threats to internal validity in Chapter 1 considered the issue of bias resulting from unequal observation or measurement of outcomes by researchers and participants.

• Attrition

Finally, there is the problem of attrition. Participants may drop out of the trial or be lost to follow-up for a variety of reasons. While there are statistical techniques for estimating missing data, the question of whether the attrition is a result of the treatment remains. In that case, as in the previous example from Chapter 1 of the antidepressant with unpleasant side effects, attrition is selective and occurs more in a specific treatment group than in the control group or groups receiving other types of treatment. Thus, bias enters into the study. This is another reason why practical steps to assure participant compliance and the collection of complete follow-up information are so important. Of course, if an intervention is so unpleasant or a treatment too complicated for a significant number of participants to follow, the intervention and the study may not be realistic to begin with.

---

* By the use of a statistical technique called analysis of covariance or ANCOVA.

Many epidemiologists believe that investigators should always analyze clinical trial data using a principle known as **intention to treat**. Intention to treat means that all study participants are included in the analysis whether or not they complete the course of treatment. In the preceding example, rates of clinical depression at the study endpoint among patients receiving the antidepressant with the unpleasant side effects would vary depending on whether dropouts were included or excluded from the analysis. An easy way to remember this idea is "once randomized, always analyzed."[12] Analysis by intention to treat is the only way to reap the full benefit of random assignment in estimating the true effect of an intervention.

Experimental studies provide the most direct evidence of a valid cause and effect relationship between treatment and outcome, with the clinical trial providing the strongest indication. The before-and-after study design poses some problems, such as overestimation of treatment effect size, but it can contribute useful data that is valuable in developing more rigorous studies.

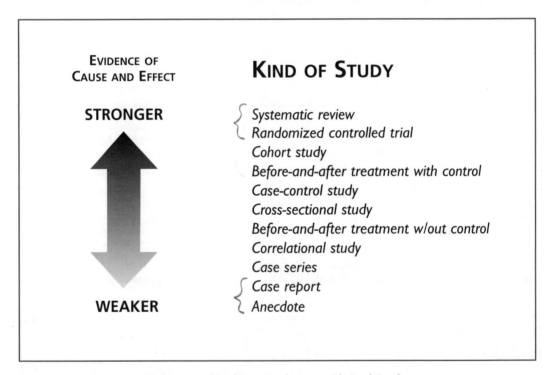

Figure 3.2 Weighting Evidence in Clinical Studies

Questions on test for sure: ex) which in stronger?
know top 2 & bottom 2

→ alphabetical

Summary

In health care research, each type of study has its own merits, its own advantages and disadvantages, its own appropriate applications, and the potential to contribute to scientific knowledge. Each provides a certain type of evidence. The important questions for the reader to consider are whether the design is consistent with the hypothesis being tested and whether the study conclusions are justified by the weight and kind of evidence presented.

The reader who can identify study designs and understand the relative strengths and weaknesses of each type is alert to the key issues to be examined when evaluating a published study. No study is perfect. Scrutinized closely enough, any study will reveal flaws and limitations. The crucial issue is whether and to what extent a flaw in the design or conduct of a study is so great that it provides a plausible alternative explanation (such as chance, bias, or confounding) for its findings, casting reasonable doubt on the authors' conclusions.

Exercises

1. Locate and read the abstract for the following review article: Ernst E., "Massage Therapy for Low Back Pain: A Systematic Review," Journal of Pain and Symptom Management, 1999 Jan; 17(1): 65-69. Compare it to the abstract for the Cochrane review on low back pain. What difference between the two reviews do you notice immediately?

2. Describe the differences between a correlational study, a case-control study, and a cohort study.

3. What questions are helpful to keep in mind when evaluating a clinical trial?

4. How do you decide whether participants in a clinical trial were randomly assigned to group(s)?

5. In any study, careful reading will discover problems. What is the crucial issue in deciding whether a study is too seriously flawed to be useful?

References

1. Montague A. *Touching: The Significance of the Human Skin.* 2nd edition. New York: Harper Books; 1978.

2. Field T. **Massage Therapy Effects.** *American Psychologist.* 1998; 53(12): 1270-1281.

3. Keenan P. **Benefits of Massage Therapy and Use of a Doula during Labor and Childbirth.** *Alternative Therapies in Health and Medicine.* 2000; 6(1): 66-74.

4. Vickers A, Ohlsson A, Lacy JB, Horsley A. *Massage for Promoting Growth and Development of Preterm and/or Low Birthweight Infants (Cochrane Review).* In: The Cochrane Library, 4, 2000. Oxford: Update Software.

5. Furlan AD, Brosseau L, Welch V, Wong J. *Massage for Low Back Pain (Cochrane Review).* In: The Cochrane Library, 4, 2000. Oxford: Update Software.

6. Slavin RE. **Best Evidence Synthesis: An Intelligent Alternative to Meta-analysis.** *Journal of Clinical Epidemiology.* 1995; 48(1): 9-18.

7. Hutchinson B. **Critical Appraisal of Review Articles.** *Canadian Family Physician.* 1993; 39: 1097-1102.

8. Centers for Disease Control. **Kaposi's Sarcoma and Pneumocystis Pneumonia Among Homosexual Men—New York City and California.** *Morbidity and Mortality Weekly Report.* Jul 3 1981; 30(25): 305-308.

9. Friedman GD. **Cigarette Smoking and Geographic Variation in Coronary Heart Disease Mortality in the United States.** *Journal of Chronic Diseases.* 1967; 20(10): 769-779.

10. Morse JM, Field PA. *Qualitative Research Methods for Health Professionals.* Thousand Oaks, CA: Sage Publications; 1995.

11. Schneider C, Jonas W. **Are Alternative Treatments Effective? Issues and Methods Involved in Measuring Effectiveness of Alternative Treatments.** *Subtle Energies.* 1994; 5(1): 69-92.

12. Hennekens CH, Buring JE. *Epidemiology in Medicine.* Boston: Little, Brown and Company; 1987.

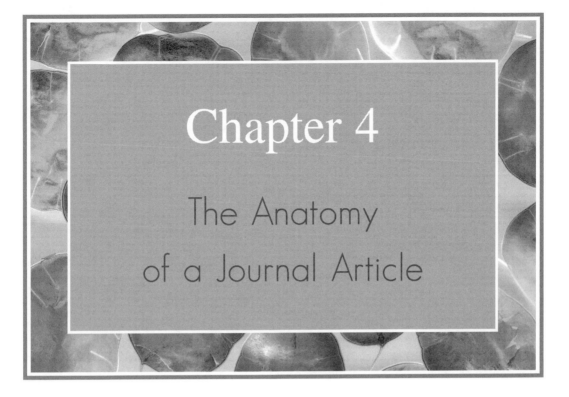

Chapter 4

The Anatomy
of a Journal Article

*A good tutor taught the whole of his subject and not just that part of it
in which he himself happened to be especially interested or proficient;
to "teach" did not, of course, mean to "impart factual information,"
a relatively unimportant consideration, but rather
to guide thought and reading and encourage reflection.*

P. B. Medawar

Learning Objectives

- Name the six sections of a journal article.

- Describe two primary functions of each section.

- Recognize the essential component(s) of each section.

Just as the practice of the health care professions requires a working knowledge of the anatomy and physiology of the human body, critical examination of a research article requires identification and study of its various components. Having clarified the logic and basic concepts that form the foundation of scientific thinking, we will now begin to narrow our focus by examining the elements that are common to any clinical research article. A typical journal article has six sections:

- the abstract
- the introduction
- the methods
- the results
- the discussion or conclusion
- the references

A related element is the author/article information, describing the institutional affiliations of the authors and sources of financial support for the study.

This chapter provides an overview of the structure and function of each journal article component. In this instance, a survey will be used as the study example, while in subsequent chapters we will scrutinize clinical trials. The questions in this chapter are intended as food for thought as you read–don't be concerned about being able to answer them in detail. At this point, the goal is to get you to begin thinking critically. A step-by-step protocol for analyzing journal articles will be laid out in the next chapters, providing a road map for more detailed examination. This chapter will start the process by using a classic study in the area of complementary medicine as an illustrative example: the 1998 Eisenberg survey on the prevalence of alternative medicine use in the United States. Several of the terms and concepts in the article were covered in Chapter 3; you may feel the need to go back and review some items as you are reading.

The Abstract

The abstract is the first section of a journal article. It functions as an executive summary of the article's contents, containing the core information on which the article is reporting. Ideally, it uses an abbreviated format and includes:

- a statement of the background or context of the study
- the purpose of the study or the research objective
- a simple description of the research design
- a description of the methodology, or how the research was carried out
- the results
- the conclusion(s) of the authors

Each topic is normally summarized in one or two sentences. In some fields, for example the social sciences, abstracts may be written in a more narrative format or may be a repetition of the first paragraph of the article. An abstract should always be a single page or less in length, yet it should convey enough information for the reader to determine whether he or she is interested in reading the full text of the article. The length and format of an abstract also varies according to the specific requirements of the journal in which it is published.

In recent years, quantitative health care literature has generally adopted what is known as a standardized abstract, using a common format as illustrated in the example that follows. Standardized abstracts provide core information in a consistent manner, making it easier to quickly identify essential information (such as the type of study design or outcome measures used) and to compare information across different articles. Notice the headings in the Eisenberg study abstract below, which are typically used in the standardized abstract. While most of the sections are admirably succinct, the results section tends to go into considerable detail.

As you read this sample abstract, consider the following questions:

1. **Do you think the authors have provided a brief summary that is readily scanned?**

2. **Have they provided enough pertinent detail to capture your interest and lead you to read the full text?**

Trends in Alternative Medicine Use in the United States, 1990-1997 Results of a Follow-up National Survey

David M. Eisenberg, MD; Roger B. Davis, ScD; Susan L. Ettner, PhD; Scott Appel, MS; Sonja Wilkey; Maria Van Rompay; Ronald C. Kessler, PhD

Context: *A prior national survey documented the high prevalence and costs of alternative medicine use in the United States in 1990.*

Objective: *To document trends in alternative medicine use in the United States between 1990 and 1997.*

Design: *Nationally representative random household telephone surveys using comparable key questions were conducted in 1991 and 1997 measuring utilization in 1990 and 1997, respectively.*

Participants: *A total of 1539 adults in 1991 and 2055 in 1997.*

Main Outcome Measures: *Prevalence, estimated costs, and disclosure of alternative therapies to physicians.*

Results: *Use of at least 1 of 16 alternative therapies during the previous year increased from 33.8% in 1990 to 42.1% in 1997 (P≤ .001). The therapies increasing the most included herbal medicine, massage, megavitamins, self-help groups, folk remedies, energy healing, and homeopathy. The probability of users visiting an alternative medicine practitioner increased from 36.3% to 46.3% (P=.002). In both surveys alternative therapies were used most frequently for chronic conditions, including back problems, anxiety, depression, and headaches. There was no significant change in disclosure rates between the 2 survey years; 39.8% of alternative therapies were disclosed to physicians in 1990 vs 38.5% in 1997. The percentage of users paying entirely out-of-pocket for services provided by alternative medicine practitioners did not change significantly between 1990 (64.0%) and 1997 (58.3%) (P=.36). Extrapolations to the US population suggest a 47.3% increase in total visits to alternative medicine practitioners, from 427 million in 1990 to 629 million in 1997, thereby exceeding total visits to all US primary care physicians. An estimated 15 million adults in 1997 took prescription medications concurrently with herbal remedies and/or high-dose vitamins (18.4% of all prescription users). Estimated expenditures for alternative medicine professional services increased 45.2% between 1990 and 1997 and were conservatively estimated at $21.2 billion in 1997, with at least $12.2 billion paid out-of-pocket. This exceeds the 1997 out-of-pocket expenditures for all US hospitalizations. Total 1997 out-of-pocket expenditures relating to alternative therapies were conservatively estimated at $27.0 billion, which is comparable with the projected 1997 out-of-pocket expenditures for all US physician services.*

Conclusions: *Alternative medicine use and expenditures increased substantially between 1990 and 1997, attributable primarily to an increase in the proportion of the population seeking alternative therapies, rather than increased visits per patient.*

Journal of the American Medical Association. 1998; 280: 1569-1575

The Introduction

The introduction states the general purpose for conducting the research study and the specific research question that the study has attempted to answer. In addition, it should include a discussion of previous literature pertinent to the question, referred to as a review of the literature. This review places the current study into the context of prior related research and provides the rationale for pursuing the study at this time. Notice that of the 29 citations listed in the Eisenberg study references, 14 of them occur in this section. Gaps in the previous literature can be identified as a support for the study rationale. A well-written introduction answers the question "Why should anyone care?" In other words, why should anyone bother to study this particular research question, and why should anyone else be interested in the results?

As you read the study's introduction, reflect on these questions:

1. Have the authors stated the purpose of the study clearly?

2. Is a review of the literature contained in the introduction?

3. How well do you think the authors make their case for the importance of conducting this survey?

Introduction: *Alternative medical therapies, functionally defined as interventions neither taught widely in medical schools nor generally available in US hospitals,[1] have attracted increased national attention from the media, the medical community, governmental agencies, and the public. A 1990 national survey of alternative medicine prevalence, costs, and patterns of use[1] demonstrated that alternative medicine has a substantial presence in the US health care system. Data from a survey in 1994[2] and a public opinion poll in 1997[3] confirmed the extensive use of alternative medical therapies in the United States. An increasing number of US insurers and managed care organizations now offer alternative medicine programs and benefits[4]. The majority of US medical schools now offer courses on alternative medicine.[5]*

National surveys performed outside the United States suggest that alternative medicine is popular throughout the industrialized world.[6] The percentage of the population who used alternative therapies during the prior 12 months has been estimated to be 10% in Denmark (1987),[7] 33% in Finland (1982),[8] and 49% in Australia (1993).[9] Public opinion polls and consumers' association surveys suggest high prevalence rates throughout Europe and the United Kingdom.[10-13] The percentage of the Canadian population who saw an alternative therapy practitioner during the previous 12 months has been estimated at 15% (1995).[14] The wide range of utilization rates can be explained, in part, by the disparity in definitions of alternative therapy and the selection of therapies assessed.

The presumption is that alternative medicine use in the United States has increased at a considerable pace in recent years. The purpose of this follow-up national survey was to investigate this presumption and document trends in alternative medicine prevalence, costs, disclosure of use to physicians, and correlates of use since 1990.

Methods and Procedures

The methods section of an article is one of the most important in terms of gauging the possibility that chance or bias have affected the study's results. This section describes in detail exactly how the study was carried out. Careful reading should reveal whether other explanations for the study results are possible. In particular, the reader should closely examine details about how participants were selected, how random assignment was performed, how abstract concepts (for example, anxiety or patriotism) were defined in terms of observable and measurable behaviors, and exactly what procedures were followed. For studies that evaluate or test the effectiveness of complementary therapies, the protocol for the treatment should be looked at in terms of its appropriateness to the research question.

With surveys and interviews, the way in which questions are worded and the order in which questions are asked can make a great deal of difference to how participants respond. While journal space rarely permits the full text of a scripted interview or questionnaire to be included, authors may disclose the wording of particular questions, especially if the results are surprising or controversial, to demonstrate that they have not tried to manipulate the responses.

Another issue to consider when evaluating a survey is this: to what degree is the sample of survey respondents representative of the entire population to which the results will be generalized? In most countries, sufficient demographic information exists so that researchers can select a sample that will duplicate these characteristics accurately and proportionally. The rate of nonresponse is also important to consider, since those who complete the surveys (respondents) can differ from those who do not (nonrespondents) in ways that affect the survey results. If only 50% of a sample actually complete the survey, the findings may not prove useful because too much information is missing.

In the Eisenberg study methods section, notice the degree of detail used to describe the methods and procedures that were followed in conducting all phases of the survey. If a term is used that you don't understand, first see if you can figure it out from the context in which it is used, then look it up. Don't worry too much about the description of how the statistical analysis was performed–we'll go into more detail on this topic in the next chapter.

As you read this section, consider your answers to the following questions:

1. **What do you think of the authors' efforts to ensure that the sample was representative of the US population?**

2. **What do you think of the description of the telephone interview?**

3. **Are you comfortable with the description/definition of some of the alternative therapies included in the survey?**

4. **Do you think that the authors took adequate precautions to avoid introducing bias?**

Methods (Sample): *We conducted parallel nationally representative telephone surveys in 1991 and 1997. Survey methods were approved by the Beth Israel Deaconess Institutional Review Board, Boston, Mass. Both surveys used random-digit dialing to select households and random selection of 1 household resident, aged 18 years or older, as the respondent. Eligibility was limited to English speakers in whom cognitive or physical impairment did not prevent completion of the interview. We asked respondents about their use of alternative therapies during the prior 12 months. We consider the results of the 1991 survey, fielded between January and March of that year, representative of 1990, and the results of the 1997 survey, fielded between November 1997 and February 1998, representative of 1997.*

The sampling scheme was designed with a target sample of 1500 in 1990 and 2000 in 1997. The latter sample size was chosen to provide power in excess of 80% to detect an increase from 34% to 39% in the proportion of adults who used at least 1 form of alternative therapy during the prior 12 months. The actual numbers of completed interviews were 1539 in 1990 (67% response rate) and 2055 in 1997 (60% weighted response rate). A secular trend in lower survey response required us to offer a $20 financial incentive for participation in the 1997 survey to maintain a response rate near the one achieved in 1990. No financial incentive was used in the 1990 survey.

The data in each survey were separately weighted to adjust for geographic variation in cooperation (e.g., by region of country and urbanicity) and for household variation in probability of selection (i.e., the inverse relationship between size of household and probability of selection because only 1 interview was completed in each sample household). The data were then weighted in parallel on sociodemographic variables to adjust for aggregate discrepancies between the sample distributions and population distributions provided by the US Census Bureau. This last stage of weighting was based on the 1997 Current Population Survey data[15] and was done in parallel across the 2 surveys to remove any between-survey discrepancies of weighted sociodemographic distributions.

Of the initial sample of 9750 telephone numbers in 1997, 26% were nonworking, 17% were not assigned to households, and 9% were unavailable (i.e., despite 6 attempted follow-up contacts). We declared 481 households ineligible because respondents did not speak English or because of cognitive or physical incapacity. Among the remaining 4167 eligible respondents, 1720 (41.3%) completed the interview on initial request. Attempts were then made to convert a random subsample of 1066 refusers by offering them an increased stipend ($50). A total of 335 (31.4%) of the 1066 contacted were converted in this manner. Extrapolating this conversion rate to all of the refusers and weighting the data for the undersampling of initial refusers, we obtained a 60% (41.3% + [31.4% x (100% - 41.3%)]) weighted overall response rate among eligible respondents.

Interview: *In both years, the interview was presented as a survey conducted about the health care practices of Americans by investigators from Harvard Medical School. No mention was made of alternative or complementary therapies. The substantive questions began by asking about perceived health, health worries, days spent in bed, and functional* impairment due to health problems. We then asked respondents about their interactions with a medical doctor, defined as "a medical doctor (MD) or a doctor of osteopathic medicine (DO), not a chiropractor or other nonmedical doctor." The term medical doctor was used throughout the remainder of the interview.

To document trends we explored the following: (1) Respondents in both surveys were presented with a list of common medical conditions and asked if they had experienced each of these conditions during the previous 12 months. (2) Respondents who reported more than 3 conditions were asked to identify their 3 most bothersome or serious medical conditions and were then asked about seeing a medical doctor for these principal medical conditions and about the perceived quality of these interactions. (3) Respondents were asked about their lifetime and past 12-month use of 16 alternative therapies and whether each of these therapies was used for each of the principal medical conditions.

The 1997 survey also asked about use for a representative sample of other medical conditions and expanded the list of therapies beyond the original 16 assessed in 1990. (4) We distinguished between use under the supervision of a practitioner of alternative therapy and use without such supervision. Respondents who reported supervised use were asked about their number of visits in the past 12 months to practitioners of each therapy. (5) All users of alternative therapies in 1997 who acknowledged seeing a medical doctor during the past year were then asked if they had discussed their use of each therapy with a medical doctor and, if not, why not.

Prior use of 16 targeted therapies was explored using a computer-assisted interview transcript, which included the following clarifications in both 1990 and 1997: When asking about high-dose vitamin or megavitamin therapies, interviewers made clear that the survey sought information on vitamins not including a daily vitamin or vitamin prescribed by a doctor. Prayer or spiritual healing by others was asked about separately from prayer or spiritual practice for individual health concern. Commercial diet programs were described as "the kind you have to pay for, but not including trying to lose or gain weight on your own." A lifestyle diet included examples like vegetarianism or macrobiotics. Questions regarding energy healing included examples of magnets, energy-emitting machines, or the "laying on of hands," and use of relaxation techniques was explained using the examples of meditation or the relaxation response. The remaining 9 therapies were asked about without interviewer clarification.

The 1997 survey was longer (average, 30 minutes) than the 1990 survey (average, 25 minutes) because we sought to explore a number of areas in more depth. All the important questions in the 1990 survey were repeated in 1997. These replicated questions are the focus of the current report. One major change in the 1997 survey involved replicated questions: respondents who reported using more than 3 alternative therapies were asked in-depth questions (e.g., use of a practitioner of alternative therapies, number of visits, out-of-pocket expenses, reasons for use) for all such therapies in 1990 but only for a random sample of 3 such therapies in 1997. This was required because of expansion in both the number of alternative therapies we assessed in 1997 and questions about each therapy. The 1997 data were weighted to adjust for this sampling in making comparisons with the 1990 data.

Insurance Coverage: *For each therapy for which respondents said they used services of an alternative medicine practitioner, we asked whether insurance helped pay for any of the costs of the therapy and whether the respondent paid any of the costs out-of-pocket. Based on the answers to these questions, we calculated the proportion of users of each therapy who had complete, partial, or no insurance coverage for that therapy. We also calculated the overall frequency of insurance coverage by weighting the insurance frequencies within each therapy by the proportion of all user therapies accounted for by that therapy.*

Construction of Cost Measures: *The total cost of visits to alternative medicine practitioners was calculated by multiplying the number of visits for each therapy by a per-visit price and adding the prices of the following therapies: relaxation techniques, herbal medicine, massage therapy, chiropractic care, megavitamins, self-help groups, imagery techniques, commercial diet, folk remedies, lifestyle diet, energy healing, homeopathy, hypnosis, biofeedback, and acupuncture. Out-of-pocket costs were constructed for each therapy by multiplying each user's visits by the full price of the visit if the user had no insurance coverage, by 0.2 if the user had partial insurance coverage, and by zero if insurance paid the full price of the visit. The assumption of a 20% coinsurance rate among users with partial insurance coverage should yield a conservative estimate of out-of-pocket costs, because it ignores deductibles and benefit caps and assumes that insurance benefits for alternative therapy are similar to medical coverage.*

We calculated costs based on per-visit prices chosen from typical prices paid for such services by private insurers using a Resource-Based Relative ValueScale (RBRVS)[16] system in selected states. We then recalculated costs using a second set of prices chosen partly to reflect empirical data on the out-of-pocket costs paid by the respondents, but primarily to represent conservative estimates of the per-visit cost of alternative therapies. Total costs based on this second set of prices should represent a lower bound on true expenditures.

Out-of-pocket costs of herbs, megavitamin supplements, and commercial diet products were calculated by multiplying the total population of users by the average out-of-pocket expenditures reported by respondents who used each of these products. In 1997, each respondent who used an alternative therapy was also asked, "Did you spend any additional money on things like books, classes, equipment, or any other items related to [the alternative therapy] in the past 12 months?" Out-of-pocket expenditures on these other items were calculated following the same procedures used for herbs, megavitamins, and commercial diet products, and related items were based on actual dollar amounts reported, so changes between 1990 and 1997 include inflation. To isolate the increase in the cost of practitioner visits between 1990 and 1997 solely because of the increase in the use of alternative therapies, we calculated 1990 practitioner costs using 1997 prices. The differences between the 1990 and 1997 costs of practitioner services reported are understated because they do not take into account inflation, estimated at 44% by the medical component of the Consumer Price Index.[17]

Statistical Analysis: *Analyses reported herein consist of computation of prevalence and mean estimates and comparisons of these estimates through the years. As the data in both surveys are weighted, the Taylor series method was used to compute significance tests using SUDAAN software.[18] χ^2 Tests of independence were used for comparing proportions, while t tests were used for continuous measures. Extrapolations of survey estimates to the total population were based on the assumption that there were 180 million adults living in the US household population in 1990 and 198 million in 1997.[15]*

Results

The results section is exactly that, a description of the analysis of the study data. The description can be either qualitative or quantitative and is presented as objectively as possible, neither supporting nor dismissing the hypothesis or study purpose. The results section is generally divided into two parts. The first part contains a descriptive analysis of the study participants' demographic data. In studies where groups of participants are compared to each other, analysis of the demographic data allows the reader to determine how comparable participants were to one another and whether there were any existing differences among the participants that might have influenced the results.

The second part contains an analysis of the outcome data. This analysis may be presented in a variety of formats, such as tables, charts, or graphs, along with a verbal description. Visual presentation of the outcome data allows the reader to see at a glance whether any statistically significant differences among groups of participants are present, and is often easier to grasp intuitively than the written description. Ideally, any visual display functions as a quantitative summary of the study's information, clearly labeled and easy to understand. As you are practicing how to read this section of an article, you may find it helpful to look at the tables first in order to get a general picture of the overall results. Then read the written explanation of results in the text. Go back to the tables again and see if they are now clearer to you.

As you continue reading the Eisenberg study, consider the following:

1. How would you rate the tables and figures in this section in terms of clarity and ease of understanding?

2. Which do you find easier to understand at first glance, the tables or the written explanation in the text?

3. What were the three most commonly used alternative therapies in 1997 for treating principal medical conditions?

4. How much money did Americans spend in out-of-pocket payments to alternative practitioners in 1997?

Results

Characteristics of Respondents: *The characteristics of the subjects we interviewed are shown in Table 1. The sociodemographic characteristics of the survey sample are similar to the population distributions published by the US Bureau of the Census.*[15]

Table 1.—Characteristics of the 1997 (N = 2055) and 1990 (N = 1539) Subjects Interviewed Compared With the US Population*

Characteristic	1997 Survey, %	1997 US Bureau of the Census,[17] %	1990 Survey, %
Sex			
Female	52	52	48
Male	48	48	52
Age, y			
18-24	10	13	16
25-34	22	20	23
35-49	33	32	27
≥50	35	35	34
Race/ethnicity			
White	77	73	82
African American	8	12	9
Hispanic	10	11	6
Asian	1	4	1
Other	4	1	2
Education			
<High school	14	18	24
High school graduate	37	34	35
College or more	49	48	40
Annual income, $			
<20000	27	33	30
20000-49999	45	41	53
≥50000	27	26	18
Region			
Northeast	21	19	22
North central	24	24	32
South	35	35	26
West	20	22	19

*Due to rounding, percentages do not always total 100.

Patterns of Use: *Use of alternative therapies in 1997 was not confined to any narrow segment of society. Rates of use ranged from 32% to 54% in the wide range of sociodemographic groups examined. Use was more common among women (48.9%) than men (37.8%) (P=.001) and less common among African Americans (33.1%) than members of other racial groups (44.5%) (P=.004). People aged 35 to 49 years reported higher rates of use (50.1%) than people either older (39.1%) (P=.001) or younger (41.8%) (P=.003). Use was higher among those who had some college education (50.6%) than with no college education (36.4%) (P=.001) and more common among people with annual incomes above $50,000 (48.1%) than with lower incomes (42.6%) (P=.03). Use was more common among those in the West (50.1%) than elsewhere in the United States (42.1%) (P=.004). With the exception of observed sex differences in 1997, these patterns are consistent with those identified in 1990.*

Population prevalence estimates of alternative medicine use in 1990 and 1997 are shown in Table 2. The 1990 survey estimated that 33.8% of the US adult population (60 million people) used at least 1 of the 16 alternative therapies listed, while the 1997 survey estimated that this proportion increased significantly to 42.1% (83 million people). A comparison of specific therapies in the first column shows increases in 15 of the16 therapies;10 of these were statistically significant (P≤ .05). The largest increases were in the use of herbal medicine, massage, megavitamins, self-help groups, folk remedies, energy healing, and homeopathy. Summing Table 2 (first column) data shows a 65% increase in total number of therapies used, from 577 therapies per 1000 population in 1990 to 953 per 1000 in 1997.

Several categories of alternative therapy warrant clarification about the actual modalities used. Three quarters of respondents who acknowledged use of relaxation techniques said

Table 2.—Comparison of Prevalence and Frequency of Use of Alternative Therapies Among Adult Respondents, 1997 vs 1990*

Type of Therapy	Used in Past 12 mo, %		Saw a Practitioner in Past 12 mo, %		Mean No. of Visits per User in Past 12 mo		No. of Visits per 1000 Population		Estimated Total No. of Visits in 1997 (in Thousands)†	Total Visits, %‡§
	1997	1990	1997	1990	1997	1990	1997	1990		
Relaxation techniques	16.3¶	13.1	15.3	9.0	20.9	18.6	521.2	219.3	103 203	16.4
Herbal medicine	12.1**	2.5	15.1	10.2	2.9	8.1	53.0	20.7	10 491	1.7
Massage	11.1**	6.9	61.6#	41.4	8.4	14.8	574.4	422.8	113 723	18.1
Chiropractic	11.0	10.1	89.9**	71.1	9.8	12.6	969.1¶	904.8	191 886	30.5
Spiritual healing by others‖	7.0#	4.2	...	9.2	...	14.2	...	54.9	...	...
Megavitamins	5.5**	2.4	23.7	11.8	8.6	12.6	112.1	35.7	22 196	3.5
Self-help group	4.8**	2.3	44.4	38.3	18.9	20.5	402.8	180.6	79 754	12.7
Imagery	4.5	4.2	23.1	15.1	11.0	14.2	114.3	90.1	22 640	3.6
Commercial diet	4.4	3.9	43.2	24.0	7.3	20.7	138.8	193.8	27 474	4.4
Folk remedies	4.2**	0.2	6.2	0.0	1.0	...	2.6	...	516	0.1
Lifestyle diet	4.0	3.6	8.0	12.5	2.8	8.1	9.0	36.5	1774	0.3
Energy healing	3.8**	1.3	26.3	32.2	20.2#	8.3	201.9¶	34.7	39 972	6.4
Homeopathy	3.4**	0.7	16.5	31.7	1.6	6.1	9.0	13.5	1777	0.3
Hypnosis	1.2	0.9	62.7	51.8	2.8	2.6	21.1	12.1	4171	0.7
Biofeedback	1.0	1.0	54.3	20.8	3.6	6.4	19.5	13.3	3871	0.6
Acupuncture	1.0¶	0.4	87.6	91.3	3.1	38.4	27.2	140.2	5377	0.9
≥1 of 16 alternative therapies	42.1**	33.8	46.3#	36.3	16.3	19.2	3176.0	2373.0	628 825	...
SE	1.2	1.4	1.9	2.5	1.8	4.5	378.7	599.7	74 997	...
Self-prayer‖	35.1**	25.2	...	...	...	...	...	...	...	...

*Percentages are of those who used that type of therapy. Ellipses indicate data not applicable.
†Estimate based on 1997 population estimate of 198 million.
‡Percentage of total visits of the 16 therapies (ie, excluding self-prayer).
§Because of rounding, percentages do not total 100.
‖Respondents who received spiritual healing by others were not asked for details of visits in 1997, nor were those who used self-prayer in either year.
¶ P≤.05; # P≤.01; ** P≤.001.

they used meditation. Among those who reported using energy healing, the most frequently cited technique involved the use of magnets. Other modalities common to this category included Therapeutic Touch, Reiki, and energy healing by religious groups. The use of self-prayer, in contrast to spiritual or energy healing performed by others, was investigated in terms of prevalence of use but not in terms of costs, referral patterns, or insurance reimbursement. All analyses in this article exclude data involving self-prayer.

Table 2 (second column) shows that a significantly higher proportion of alternative therapy users saw an alternative medicine practitioner in 1997 (46.3%; equivalent to 39 million people) than in 1990 (36.3%, equivalent to 22 million people). Of the 15 therapies for which the question was asked, the proportion of users who saw a practitioner increased for 11. However, even in 1997 there were only 5 therapies in which a majority of users consulted a practitioner: massage, chiropractic, hypnosis, biofeedback, and acupuncture. Unsupervised use (i.e., a form of expanded self-care) remains the usual method of use for all other alternative therapies.

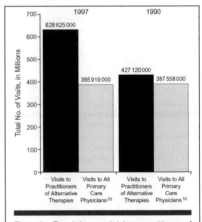

Figure 1.—Trends in annual visits to practitioners of alternative therapies vs visits to primary care physicians, United States, 1997 vs 1990. Data are from the National Ambulatory Medical Care Survey from 1996[20] and 1990.[19]

Making Sense of Research

Table 2 (third column) reveals no consistent change in the average number of visits among respondents who consulted practitioners of alternative therapy between 1990 (19.2%) and 1997 (16.3%). However, because of the increase in the proportion of people using these therapies, the total number of visits increased substantially from 1990 to 1997. This 47.3% increase in total visits is largely because of increases in visits for relaxation therapy, massage, chiropractic, self-help, and energy healing. The visits to practitioners of alternative therapy in 1997 exceeded the projected number of visits to all primary care physicians in the United States by an estimated 243 million (Figure 1).[19,20] Visits to chiropractors and massage therapists accounted for nearly half of all visits to practitioners of alternative therapies.

Prevalence estimates for selected additional therapies assessed in 1997 but not 1990 include: aromatherapy (5.6%), neural therapy (1.7%), naturopathy (0.7%), and chelation therapy (0.13%) (data not shown). Comparisons of total visits and costs for 1990 and 1997 were performed without inclusion of these data. Prevalence estimates for the simultaneous use of prescription medication with herbs, with high-dose vitamins, or with both were obtained. Among the 44% of adults who said they regularly take prescription medications, nearly 1 (18.4%) in 5 reported the concurrent use of at least 1 herbal product, a high-dose vitamin, or both.

Table 3.—Comparison of Use of Alternative Therapies for the Most Frequently Reported Principal Medical Conditions, 1997 vs 1990

Condition	Percentage Reporting Condition		Used Alternative Therapy for Condition in Past 12 mo, %		Saw Alternative Practitioner for Condition in Past 12 mo, %		Saw Medical Doctor and Used Alternative Therapy for Condition in Past 12 mo, %		Saw Medical Doctor and Alternative Practitioner for Condition in Past 12 mo, %		Therapies Most Commonly Used in 1997
	1997	1990	1997	1990	1997	1990	1997	1990	1997	1990	
Back problems	24.0#	19.9	47.6#	35.9	30.1#	19.5	58.8**	36.1	39.1#	23.0	Chiropractic, massage
Allergies	20.7#	16.0	16.6#	8.7	4.2	3.3	28.0¶	15.7	6.4	5.0	Herbal, relaxation
Fatigue*	16.7	...	27.0	...	6.3	...	51.6	...	13.1	...	Relaxation, massage
Arthritis	16.6	15.9	26.7¶	17.5	10.0	7.6	38.5¶	23.8	15.9	13.8	Relaxation, chiropractic
Headaches	12.9	13.2	32.2	26.5	13.3¶	6.3	42.0	31.8	20.0	12.1	Chiropractic, relaxation
Neck problems*	12.1	...	57.0	...	37.5	...	66.6	...	47.5	...	Chiropractic, massage
High blood pressure	10.9	11.0	11.7	11.0	0.9	2.9	11.9	11.6	1.1	3.5	Megavitamins, relaxation
Sprains or strains	10.8	13.4	23.6	22.3	10.3	9.6	29.4	24.7	15.9	13.6	Chiropractic, relaxation
Insomnia	9.3#	13.6	26.4	20.4	7.6	4.0	48.4	19.8	13.3	10.9	Relaxation, herbal
Lung problems	8.7	7.3	13.2	8.8	2.5	0.5	17.9	11.1	3.4	0.6	Relaxation, spiritual healing, herbal
Skin problems	8.6	8.0	6.7	6.0	2.2	1.6	6.8	6.9	0.0	2.5	Imagery, energy healing
Digestive problems	8.2	10.1	27.3#	13.2	9.7¶	3.6	34.1¶	15.3	10.7	5.8	Relaxation, herbal
Depression†	5.6	8.4	40.9	20.2	15.6	7.0	40.9	35.2	26.9	14.0	Relaxation, spiritual healing
Anxiety‡	5.5	9.5	42.7	27.9	11.6	6.5	42.7	45.4	21.0	10.4	Relaxation, spiritual healing
Weighted average across all conditions§	...	...	28.2**	19.1	11.4**	6.8	31.8**	19.9	13.7#	8.3	...
People with ≥1 condition‖	77.8¶	81.5	33.7**	22.9	15.3**	6.9	...	...	...	...	...

*Not included as a separate question in 1990 survey. Ellipses indicate data not applicable.
†The 1997 question asked about severe depression, which is not directly comparable with the 1990 question that asked about depression.
‡The 1997 question asked about anxiety attacks, which is not directly comparable with the 1990 question that asked about anxiety.
§The weighted averages are calculated based on all 37 conditions studied in 1997 and all 24 conditions studied in 1990, ie, condition is unit of analysis.
‖This row shows percentage of respondents who reported 1 or more principal medical conditions, along with the percentage of these respondents who reported use of therapy or practitioners for at least 1 of these conditions, ie, person is the unit of analysis.
¶ P≤.05; # P≤.01; ** P<.001.

© 1998 American Medical Association

Table 3 summarizes results regarding use of alternative therapies for the most commonly reported principal medical conditions in either survey. In each year; a majority of respondents reported 1 or more principal medical conditions. The list of conditions was expanded in 1997 (37 conditions) compared with 1990 (24 conditions). Significant increases in the proportion using alternative therapies for principal condition(s) (second column) occurred for back problems, allergies, arthritis, and digestive problems. The highest condition-specific rates of alternative therapy use in 1997 were for neck (57.0%) and back (47.6%) problems. The proportion of respondents with 1 or more medical conditions who reported use of an alternative therapy for at least 1 of those conditions increased significantly from 22.9% in 1990 to 33.7% in 1997 (P≤ .001). The weighted condition-specific proportion who saw an alternative medicine practitioner for a given condition also increased significantly from 6.8% in 1990 to 11.4% in 1997 (P≤ .001).

Table 3 also summarizes the probability that individuals who saw a medical doctor for a particular condition also used an alternative therapy (fourth column) or also saw a practitioner of alternative therapy (fifth column) for that same condition during the same year. A generally increasing pattern of alternative medicine use can be seen across the range of conditions studied. In 1990, an estimated 1 (19.9%) in 5 individuals seeing a medical doctor for a principal condition also used an alternative therapy. This percentage increased to nearly 1 (31.8%) in 3 in 1997 (P≤ .001). The percentage who saw a medical doctor and also sought the services of an alternative practitioner increased significantly from 8.3% in 1990 to 13.7% in 1997 (P≤ .01). In both 1990 and 1997, chiropractic, relaxation techniques, and massage therapy were among the alternative therapies used most commonly to treat principal medical conditions.

As in 1990, 96% of 1997 respondents who saw a practitioner of alternative therapy for a principal condition also saw a medical doctor during the prior 12 months, and only a minority of alternative therapies used were discussed with a medical doctor. Among the 618 respondents in 1997 who used 1 or more alternative therapies and had a medical doctor, only 377 (38.5%) of the 979 therapies used were discussed with the respondent's medical doctor. This is not significantly different from the 353 (39.8%) of the 886 therapies discussed by the comparable group of respondents (n=501) in the 1990 survey. Given that most alternative therapy is used without the supervision of an alternative practitioner, a substantial portion of alternative therapy use for principal medical conditions (46.0% in 1997 and 51.3% in 1990) was done without input from either a medical doctor or practitioner of alternative therapy.

Payment for Alternative Therapy: Data on insurance coverage of expenditures for alternative therapy services are shown in Table 4. The majority of people who saw alternative therapy practitioners paid all the costs out-of-pocket in both 1990 (64.0%) and 1997 (58.3%). None of the changes in insurance coverage between 1990 and 1997 were statistically significant, probably due in part to small sample sizes.

Using conservative assumptions about the fees charged by practitioners of alternative therapies and assuming no changes in visit prices, Americans spent an estimated $14.6

Table 4.—Insurance Coverage of Alternative Medicine Services in the United States, 1997 vs 1990*

	Percentage of Users of Services					
	Coverage, 1997			Coverage, 1990		
Type of Therapy	Complete	Partial	None	Complete	Partial	None
Relaxation techniques	28.8	6.6	64.7	5.3	25.9	68.7
Herbal medicine	8.6	11.2	80.2	30.7	15.5	53.8
Massage	11.8	16.7	71.5	19.1	18.3	62.6
Chiropractic	17.6	38.1	44.3	11.5	32.8	55.9
Spiritual healing by others†	...	...	...	0.0	0.0	100.0
Megavitamins	2.7	53.3	44.0	0.0	100.0	0.0
Self-help group	11.7	36.9	51.5	2.8	17.4	79.8
Imagery	51.5	3.5	45.0	16.1	0.0	83.9
Commercial diet	5.0	40.1	54.9	0.0	5.1	94.9
Folk remedies	0.0	0.0	100.0	...	...	...
Lifestyle diet	0.0	44.9	55.1	62.3	0.0	37.7
Energy healing	30.8	8.2	61.1	0.0	19.1	80.9
Homeopathy	0.0	0.0	100.0	0.0	24.7	75.3
Hypnosis	5.1	0.0	94.9	7.0	0.0	93.0
Biofeedback	30.5	43.7	26.0	14.1	19.9	66.0
Acupuncture	0.0	40.7	59.3	21.6	23.0	55.4
Weighted average across all therapies	15.3	26.4	58.3	12.3	23.7	64.0

*Data are percentage of users of alternative therapies provided by practitioners. Ellipses indicate data not applicable.

†Reimbursement patterns not explored in 1997.

© 1998 American Medical Association

billion on visits to these practitioners in 1990 and $21.2 billion in 1997 (Table 5). Using less conservative (RVRBS) price figures, the amount spent on services of practitioners of alternative therapies was estimated at $22.6 billion in 1990 and $32.7 billion in 1997. Regardless of which set of prices is used, total expenditures for practitioners of alternative therapies are estimated to have increased by approximately 45% between 1990 and 1997 exclusive of inflation.

Estimated out-of-pocket expenditures for high-dose vitamins increased from $0.9 billion in 1990 to $3.3 billion in 1997. Smaller increases were observed for commercial diet products ($1.3 billion vs $1.7 billion). Unlike the 1990 survey, the 1997 survey included questions about expenditures for herbal products ($5.1 billion) and respondents' alternative therapy-specific books, classes, or equipment ($4.7 billion).

The estimated total out-of-pocket component of the alternative medicine market in 1997 is shown in Figure 2. Projected out-of-pocket expenditures for all

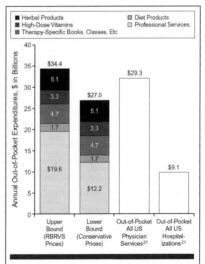

Figure 2.—Estimated annual out-of-pocket expenditures for alternative therapies vs conventional medical services, United States, 1997. Data are from the Health Care Financing Administration, United States.[21] RBRVS indicates Resource-Based Relative Value Scale.

© 1998 American Medical Association

Table 5.—National Projections of Expenditures for Alternative Therapies in the United States, 1997 vs 1990*

Category of Expenditure	1997 (Billions of Dollars)		1990 (Billions of Dollars)		Change (%), 1997 vs 1990 (Billions of Dollars)	
	Conservative (SE)	RBRVS (SE)	Conservative (SE)	RBRVS (SE)	Conservative	RBRVS
Total expenditures on professional services for 15 alternative therapies†	21.2 (2.4)	32.7 (3.8)	14.6 (4.0)	22.6 (6.1)	6.6 (45.2)	10.1 (44.7)
Out-of-pocket expenditures						
Professional services, 15 therapies†‡	12.2 (1.7)	19.6 (3.3)	7.2 (1.3)	11.0 (2.1)	5.0 (69.4)§	8.6 (78.2)§
Megavitamins	3.3 (0.4)		0.9 (0.3)		2.4 (266.7)‖	
Commercial diet products	1.7 (0.3)		1.3 (0.3)		0.4 (30.8)	
Subtotal of out-of-pocket expenditures assessed in 1997 and 1990†	17.2	24.6	9.4	13.2	7.8 (83.0)	11.4 (86.4)
Out-of-pocket expenditures assessed only in 1997						
Herbal medicine	5.1 (0.5)		...		...	
Therapy-specific books, classes, and equipment	4.7 (0.8)		...		...	
Total out-of-pocket expenditures for alternative therapies in 1997†	27.0	34.4	...	...	...	...

*The 1990 and 1997 cost measures are based on 1990 and 1997 population estimates, respectively (180 million vs 198 million). Both used 1997 per-visit price estimates as follows (conservative price estimate is followed by Resource-Based Relative Value Scale [RBRVS] estimate for each therapy): relaxation techniques ($20, $50), herbal medicine ($40, $60), massage therapy ($40, $60), chiropractic care ($40, $65), megavitamins ($40, $50), self-help groups ($20, $20), imagery techniques ($45, $50), commercial diet ($20, $20), folk remedies ($20, $50), lifestyle diet ($20, $60), energy healing ($40, $50), homeopathy ($45, $60), hypnosis ($60, $80), biofeedback ($60, $80), and acupuncture ($40, $60). (Price estimates for spiritual healing by others were not included because respondents reporting use were not asked for details of professional visits). Ellipses indicate data not applicable.

†These figures reflect the range in out-of-pocket expenditures for conservative vs RBRVS-derived visit prices.

‡Assumes a 20% copayment for users with partial insurance coverage.

§$P \leq .05.$; ‖$P \leq .001.$

© 1998 American Medical Association

hospitalizations in 1997 in the United States totaled $9.1 billion, while projected out-of-pocket expenses for all US physician services in the same year were $29.3 billion.[21] This compares to a conservatively estimated $12.2 billion in out-of-pocket payments to alternative medicine practitioners for the 15 therapies studied. Adding the estimates of $5.1 billion for herbal therapies, $3.3 billion for megavitamins, $1.7 billion for diet products, and $4.7 billion on alternative therapy-specific books, classes, and equipment, the total out-of-pocket expenditures for alternative medicine are conservatively estimated to be $27.0 billion. Using the average per-visit prices derived from an RBRVS system[16] rather than our conservative estimates (Table 5), the estimated total out-of-pocket expense is approximately $34.4 billion, which is comparable with the projected 1997 out-of-pocket expenditures for all physician services.[21] These estimates exclude out-of-pocket expenditures associated with therapies unique to the 1997 survey (e.g., naturopathy, aromatherapy, neural therapy, and chelation therapy).

Discussion of Results or Conclusion

This section answers the question, "So what do these results mean in terms of the research question?" The conclusion of an article is often the most interesting, and just like a mystery novel, many readers skip ahead and peek to see how the story ends. It is important to remember, however, that this section is based on the authors' interpretation and opinion of what the data mean. Ideally, this opinion is informed and supported by the results. Citations to other studies that are consistent with the study's findings are also helpful in bolstering the authors' case.

As you read the Eisenberg study example, notice that the authors have also included a discussion of the limitations of the study. This is usually a good indication that the authors have given thought to how widely the results can be generalized, or to the strength of the association between exposure and observed outcome.

> Consider the following questions as you continue to read:
>
> 1. **What do you think of the discussion of the study's limitations?**
>
> 2. **Do you agree with authors' construction of a 'continuum' of alternative therapies?**
>
> 3. **Do you agree with their conclusions overall?**

Comment: *The results of our study are limited by the restriction of the sampling frame to people who speak English and have telephones and by the low response rate. The decrease in overall response rate from 67% in 1990 to 60% in 1997 is consistent with secular trends for US telephone interviews in recent years.[22] It is difficult to know what, if any, bias was introduced or whether trend estimates are biased by the fact that financial incentives were used in 1997 but not 1990. Furthermore, we have no data on the accuracy of self-reports concerning recollections of number of visits and amounts spent on books, classes, relevant equipment, herbs, or supplements. To the extent possible, we adjusted by weighting data on sociodemographic variables associated with alternative therapy use (e.g., income, education, age, region). It is conceivable that the estimated prevalence and costs of alternative therapy use would have been lower if it were possible to correct for those limitations.*

Within the context of these limitations, the results of these 2 surveys suggest that the prevalence and expenditures associated with alternative medical therapies in the United States have increased substantially from 1990 to 1997. This increase appears to be primarily due to increases in the prevalence of use and in the frequency with which users of alternative therapy sought professional services. In 1997, an estimated 4 in 10 Americans used at least 1 alternative therapy as compared with 3 in 10 in 1990. For adults aged 35 to 49 years in 1997, it is estimated that 1 of every 2 persons used at least 1 alternative therapy. Overall prevalence of use increased by 25%, total visits by an estimated 47%, and expenditures on services provided by practitioners of alternative therapies by an estimated 45% exclusive of inflation. Moreover, the use of alternative therapies is distributed widely across all sociodemographic groups.

It is possible to arrange the 16 principal therapies common to the 1990 and 1997 surveys along a spectrum that varies from "more alternative" to "less alternative" in relationship to existing medical school curricula, clinical training, and practice. Arguably, therapies such as biofeedback, hypnosis, guided imagery relaxation techniques that involve elicitation of the relaxation response (<1% of the sample), lifestyle diet, and (possibly) vitamin therapy can be considered as representative of the more conventional (i.e., less alternative) side of the spectrum. Visits associated with these 6 categories accounted for less than 10% of total visits to alternative medicine practitioners; the remainder were associated with the more alternative therapies.

In light of the observed 380% increase in the use of herbal remedies and the 130% increase in high-dose vitamin use, it is not surprising to find that nearly 1 in 5 individuals taking prescription medications also was taking herbs, high-dose vitamin supplements, or both. Extrapolations to the total US population suggest that an estimated 15 million adults are at risk for potential adverse interactions involving prescription medications and herbs or high-dose vitamin supplements. This figure includes nearly 3 million adults aged 65 years or older. Adverse interactions of this nature, including alterations of drug bioavailability or efficacy, are known to occur[23-27] and are more likely among individuals with chronic medical illness, especially those with liver or kidney abnormalities. No adequate mechanism currently is in place to collect relevant surveillance data to document the extent to which the potential for drug-herb and drug-vitamin interaction is real or imaginary.

The magnitude of the demand for alternative therapy is noteworthy, in light of the relatively low rates of insurance coverage for these services. Unlike hospitalizations and physician services, alternative therapies are only infrequently included in insurance benefits. Even when alternative therapies are covered, they tend to have high deductibles and co-payments and tend to be subject to stringent limits on the number of visits or total dollar coverage. Because the demand for health care (and presumably alternative therapies) is sensitive to how much patients must pay out-of-pocket,[28] current use is likely to underrepresent utilization patterns if insurance coverage for alternative therapies increases in the future.

In 1990, a full third of respondents who used alternative therapy did not use it for any principal medical condition.[1] From these data, we inferred that a substantial amount of alternative therapy was used for health promotion or disease prevention. In 1997, 42% of all alternative therapies used were exclusively attributed to treatment of existing illness, whereas 58% were used, at least in part, to "prevent future illness from occurring or to maintain health and vitality."

Despite the dramatic increases in use and expenditures associated with alternative medical care, the extent to which patients disclose their use of alternative therapies to their physicians remains low. Less than 40% of the alternative therapies used were disclosed to a physician in both 1990 and 1997. It would be overly simplistic to blame either the patient or their physician for this inadequacy in patient-physician communication. The current status quo, which can be described as "don't ask and don't tell," needs to be abandoned.[29] Professional strategies for responsible dialogue in this area need to be further developed and refined.

Data from this survey, reflective of the US population, are representative of a predominantly white population. Even if we were to combine data sets from the 1990 and 1997 surveys, we would not have a sufficiently large database to provide precise estimates of the patterns of alternative therapy use among African Americans, Hispanic Americans, Asian Americans, or other minority groups. Parallel surveys, modified to include therapies unique to minority populations and translated when appropriate, should be conducted using necessary sampling strategies. Only then can we compare patterns across ethnic groups and prioritize research agendas for individual populations. As alternative medicine is introduced by third-party payers as an attractive insurance product, it would be unfair for individuals without health insurance and those with less expendable income to be excluded from useful alternative medical services or consultation (e.g., professional advice on use or avoidance of alternative therapies).

In conclusion, our survey confirms that alternative medicine use and expenditures have increased dramatically from 1990 to 1997. In light of these observations, we suggest that federal agencies, private corporations, foundations, and academic institutions adopt a more proactive posture concerning the implementation of clinical and basic science research, the development of relevant educational curricula, credentialing, and referral guidelines, improved quality control of dietary supplements, and the establishment of postmarket surveillance of drug-herb (and drug-supplement) interactions.

Author and Article Information

This addendum to an article describes the credentials and organizational or institutional affiliations of the author, and provides contact information for those wishing to request reprints of the article or to correspond with the lead author. Almost all peer-reviewed journals now require authors to disclose all sources of funding for the study as well, so that readers can decide whether the sources of money that supported the study may have influenced the results, in addition to the organizations or institutions that employ the authors. This section also provides a space for the authors to acknowledge the assistance of others such as research assistants who helped carry out the study, or colleagues who critiqued the manuscript. The author and article information for the Eisenberg article follows.

From the Center for Alternative Medicine Research and Education, Department of Medicine, Beth Israel Deaconess Medical Center (Drs Eisenberg and Davis, Mr Appel, and Mss Wilkey and Van Rompay), and the Department of Health Care Policy, Harvard Medical School (Drs Ettner and Kessler), Boston, Mass.

Reprints: David M. Eisenberg, MD, Center for Alternative Medicine Research and Education, Beth Israel Deaconess Medical Center, 330 Brookline Ave, Boston, MA 02215.

This study was supported in part by National Institutes of Health grant U24 AR43441, Bethesda, Md, the John E. Fetzer Institute, Kalamazoo, Mich, The American Society of Actuaries, Schaumburg, III, the Friends of Beth Israel Deaconess Medical Center, and the Kenneth J. Germeshausen Foundation, Boston, Mass, and the J. E. and Z. B. Butler Foundation, New York, NY.

The authors thank the staff of DataStat, Inc, Ann Arbor, Mich, for their assistance with telephone data collection, Linda Bedell-Logan for assistance with RBRVS data analyses, Dan Cherkin, PhD, Murray Mittleman, MD, Ted Kaptchuk, OMD, and Thomas Delbanco, MD, for their review of the manuscript, and Debora Lane, Marcia Rich, and Robb Scholten for their technical assistance.

References

The reference section of the article establishes whether and how well the author has considered the work of other researchers and scholars. The formatting for the references will vary according to the individual journal, yet it always contains sufficient information for the reader to locate the original source of the citation. The list of citations should be current in relation to the article's publication date and content. For example, if the majority of citations in an article on acupuncture and immune function are more than 15 years old, the article's concepts are likely to have been superceded because immunology is such a rapidly expanding field. The obvious exception is an article that is primarily historical in nature.

Ideally, a reference section is both relevant and succinct. Look out for the brief article with more references than text—the authors may be trying to impress you with quantity rather than quality. Equally suspicious is the speculative article with little grounding in previous studies that is notable for its lack of citations. Reference lists also provide a good resource for further exploration of a topic.

As you become knowledgeable about the literature in a given area, you will also notice whether references with which you are familiar are used appropriately. That is, does the cited article really support the author's statement? For example, an author may assert that 75% of complementary practitioners have more than 1000 hours of training in their specialty, and references another article as the basis for this statement. Is the article cited a well-designed and carefully conducted survey published by in a peer-reviewed journal, or is it an editorial in a popular magazine?

References

1. *Eisenberg DM, Kessler RC, Foster C, et al. Unconventional medicine in the United States.* N Engl J Med. *1993; 328: 246-252.*

2. *Paramore LC. Use of alternative therapies.* J Pain Symptom Manage. *1997;13: 83-89.*

3. *Landmark Healthcare.* The Landmark Report on Public Perceptions of Alternative Care. *Sacramento, Calif: Landmark Healthcare. 1998.*

4. *Pelletier KR, Marie A, Krasner M, et al. Current trends in the integration and reimbursement of complementary and alternative medicine by managed care, insurance carriers, and hospital providers.* Am J Health Promot. *1997; 12: 112-122.*

5. *Wetzel MS, Eisenberg DM, Kaptchuk TJ. Courses involving complementary and alternative medicine at US medical schools.* JAMA. *1998; 280: 784-787.*

6. *Goldbeck-Wood S, Dorozynski A, Lie LG, et al. Complementary medicine is booming worldwide.* BMJ. *1996; 313: 131-133.*

7. *Rasmussen NK Morgall JM. The use of alternative treatments in the Danish adult population.* Complementary Med Res. *1990; 4: 16-22.*

8. *Vaskilampi T Merilainen P, Sinkkonen S et al. The use of alternative treatments in the Finnish adult population. In: Lewith GT, Aldridge D, eds.* Clinical Research Methodology for Complementary Therapies. *London, England: Hodder & Stoughton; 1993: 204-229.*

9. *MacLennan AH, Wilson DH Taylor AW. Prevalence and cost of alternative medicine in Australia.* Lancet. *1996; 347: 569-573.*

10. *Fisher P, Ward A. Complementary medicine in Europe.* BMJ. *1994; 309: 107-111.*

11. *Sermeus G. Alternative health care in Belgium.* Complementary Med Res. *1990; 4: 9-13.*

12. *Bouchayer F. Alternative medicines.* Complementary Med Res. *1990; 4: 4-8.*

13. *Piel E. Erfahrungen mit Naturheilmitteln-Umfrageergebnisse aus West-und Ostdeutschland.* Therapeutikon. *1991; 5: 549-551.*

14. *Millar WJ. Use of alternative health care practitioners by Canadians.* Can J Public Health. *1997; 88: 154-158.*

15. *US Bureau of the Census. United States population estimates, by age, sex, race, and Hispanic origin,1990 to 1997. Available at: http://www.census.gov/population/estimates/nation/intfile2-1.txt.*

16. *Resource-Based Relative Value Scale Converter. Customized Report for Medical Billing and Collection of All CPT Codes. Salt Lake City, Utah: Medicode Inc; 1996.*

17. *US Bureau of Labor Statistics Data.* Consumer Price Index-All Urban Consumers. *US Bureau of Labor Statistics Web site. Available at: http://146.142.4.24/cgi-bin/surveymost?cu.1998. Series ID: CUUR0000SAM.*

18. *SUDDAAN:* Professional Software for Survey Data Analysis *[computer program]. Version 7.5. Research Triangle Park, NC: Research Triangle Institute; 1997.*

19. *Schappert SM.* National Ambulatory Medical Care Survey:1990 Summary. *Hyattsville, Md: National Center for Health Statistics, 1992. Advance Data From Vital and Health Statistics, No. 213: 1-11.*

20. *Woodwell DA.* National Ambulatory Medical Care Survey: 1996 Summary. *Hyattsville, Md: National Center for Health Statistics;1997. Advance Data From Vital and Health Statistics, No. 295: 1-25.*

21. *Health Care Financing Administration, Office of the Actuary, National Health Statistics Group. National health care expenditure projections tables. Available at: http://www.hcfa.gov/stats/NHE-Proj/tables/.*

22. *Groves RM, Couper MP. Societal environmental influences on survey participation. In:* Nonresponse in Household Interview Surveys. *New York, NY: John Wiley & Sons Inc; 1998: 159.*

23. *Ernst E. Harmless herbs?* Am J Med. *1998; 104: 170-178.*

24. *D'Arcy PF. Adverse reactions and interactions with herbal medicines, part 1: adverse reactions.* Adverse Drug React Toxicol Rev. *1991; 10: 189-208.*

25. *D'Arcy PF. Adverse reactions and interactions with herbal medicines, part 2: drug interactions.* Adverse Drug React Toxicol Rev. *1993; 12: 147-162.*

26. *De Smet PAGM, D'Arcy PF. Drug interactions with herbal and other non-orthodox remedies. In: D'Arcy PF, McElnay JC, Welling PG, eds.* Mechanisms of Drug Interactions. *New York, NY: Springer Publishing Co Inc; 1996: 327-352.*

27. *De Smet PA. Health risks of herbal remedies.* Drug Saf. *1995; 13: 81-93.*

28. *Shekelle PG, Rogers WH, Newhouse JP. The effect of cost sharing on the use of chiropractic services.* Med Care. *1996; 34: 863-872.*

29. *Elsenberg DM. Advising patients who seek alternative medical therapies.* Ann Intern Med. *1997; 127: 61-69.*

Summary

Each section of a journal article helps to create its overall structure and serves a specific function. These include: the abstract, which summarizes the article; the introduction, which states the research question and provides a review of the relevant literature; the methods and procedures, where the exact steps used to carry out the study are described; the results, which contain a visual summary and verbal description of the statistical analyses of the study data; the discussion or conclusion, where the authors discuss their interpretation of what the results mean; and the references, or citations to other published works. Familiarity with each section of an article and its purpose is a necessary step in critical evaluation.

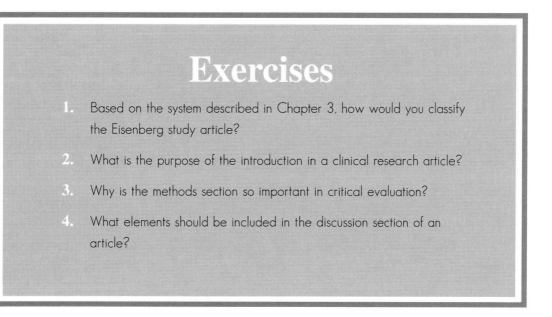

Exercises

1. Based on the system described in Chapter 3, how would you classify the Eisenberg study article?

2. What is the purpose of the introduction in a clinical research article?

3. Why is the methods section so important in critical evaluation?

4. What elements should be included in the discussion section of an article?

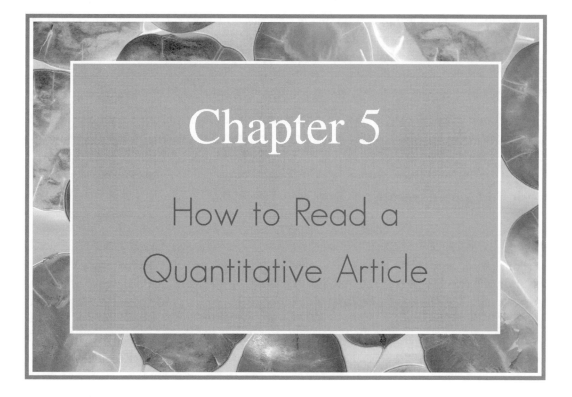

Chapter 5

How to Read a Quantitative Article

It is no kindness to a colleague–indeed, it might be the act of an enemy–to assure a scientist that his work is clear and convincing and that his opinions are really coherent when the experiments that profess to uphold them are slovenly in design and not well done. More generally, criticism is the most powerful weapon in any methodology of science; it is the scientist's only assurance that he need not persist in error.

P. B. Medawar

Learning Objectives

- Use the questions in this chapter as a guide for critical evaluation of a quantitative journal article.

- Be able to read the results section of an article with confidence.

- Differentiate between statistical and clinical significance.

- Identify the key issue involved in evaluating any journal article.

In this chapter we get down to the specifics of how one critically reads a journal article. For each section of a typical clinical research article, questions to guide your evaluation are listed. These questions are presented as a general protocol. In this chapter the intention is to familiarize the reader with a systematic approach to the critique process. In Chapter 6 we will model the use of the protocol through analyzing two different quantitative journal articles.

The questions given here are oriented toward quantitative studies, because these are by far the most numerous in the health care literature to date. Critical evaluation of qualitative studies is discussed separately in Chapter 7.

General Considerations

There are several general considerations to keep in mind as you read any article. First, remember the primary rule: *be skeptical*. When an author is making assertions or claiming statements as facts, ask yourself on what basis these claims are being made, and whether some other plausible explanation is possible. It is the author's job to provide a convincing argument based on evidence rather than persuasion or emotional appeals.

Is the journal peer-reviewed?

Another consideration is the general quality of the journal in which the article is published. Being published in a prestigious journal doesn't make an article automatically better, but articles published in journals that lack a critical peer-review system have not been subject to the same process of scrutiny and quality control. Look at the journal's guidelines for authors to determine whether submissions are treated to a blind review, that is where the reviewers do not know the authors' identities and therefore cannot be influenced by reputation or institutional affiliation. Despite the pleas of methodologists in every scientific discipline, research projects that are poorly conceived and executed are still undertaken, and articles describing their results are published somewhere every month.

The Abstract

The key question to ask here is:

What information, if any, is missing?

The abstract should contain concise statements highlighting the context of the study, the research objective, the study design, information about the participants, the main outcome measures, the results, and the researchers' conclusions. Older articles are more likely to have abstracts that lack clarity, lack sufficient detail, are missing information, or that use the first paragraph of the article as an abstract. What is missing in the abstract is your first clue as to what to look for in the rest of the article.

The Introduction

The first question to ask after reading an article's introduction is this:

Is the study objective clearly stated?

Although the abstract typically contains a statement of the study objective, the introduction should clearly elaborate the specific hypothesis being tested or the research question being investigated. If the hypothesis is vague or too general, chances are that the study results will not provide useful information. An unclear or poorly conceived hypothesis is a red flag.

The next question to ask is:

Are the study's relevance and context established?

As we mentioned in the last chapter, the purpose of the introduction is to set the stage for the rest of the article by providing a rationale for conducting this particular study and by placing the study in an historical context through a concise but pertinent discussion of past studies. If you are reading critically and find that you are persuaded of the study's importance or necessity, the authors have likely done a good job of establishing relevance. As you become more familiar with the literature in your areas of interest, you will be able to judge for yourself how well the authors have succeeded in providing a balanced and accurate summary of previous studies.

Methods and Procedures

This is the section where we really get specific. There are a number of questions to ask when evaluating the methods and procedures used in a study. If the authors have not previously specified the study design in the abstract, it should be stated here. Generally speaking, all of the questions that follow should be answered by the authors with enough information so that a reader with the requisite time, money, and expertise could reproduce the study.

Is the sample well described, including inclusion/exclusion criteria and method of selection?

Does the sample population, chosen to represent the larger population to which the results will be generalized, suit the study hypothesis? The study participants should also be described in sufficient demographic detail so that the reader can determine whether the results are likely to apply to his or her clinical practice. An explanation of the inclusion and exclusion criteria and the selection method used are necessary to help the reader judge whether the sample was chosen on the basis of convenience or whether each eligible participant had an equal chance of being selected. Without sufficient information on sampling procedures it is difficult for the reader to evaluate the possibility or degree of sampling bias, and whether it is likely to over or underestimate treatment effect.

Surveys are especially sensitive to sampling bias because the results are intended to be extrapolated to a much larger population, and a small error in the sample may be magnified many times over when projected onto the larger group. The results table will generally specify the estimated amount of possible error, called the **margin of error**, which should usually be less than 5%. In the Eisenberg study cited in Chapter 4, for example, the authors have gone to great lengths to ensure that the sample is randomly selected and representative of the US population, and that adequate demographic information is provided. The inclusion and exclusion criteria are based on common sense for a telephone survey.

Are blinding procedures used, and if so, how well did they work?

As previously discussed, blinding as a design feature helps to reduce or equalize the effect of expectation, and adds credibility to study results. Remember that with single blinding *either* participants *or* providers are blinded as to group assignment, while with double blinding both are unaware. It is important to keep in mind that efforts to blind study participants or treatment providers are not always adequate or successful. It is more impressive if the authors use a method for reflecting on how well their blinding procedures worked, for example by going back and asking whether participants had realized which group they were in.

Is a comparison or placebo group part of the design?

The inclusion of these design features helps reduce potential bias and adds credibility to study results. When evaluating the use of a comparison or placebo group in a quantitative study, the important consideration is whether the two groups are alike in every respect that may influence the outcome except the treatment or intervention being tested. This is the reason that random assignment to group is such a powerful design feature for increasing the internal validity of a study–it ensures that the groups will be similar even in terms of unanticipated characteristics that could influence outcomes to be measured.

For an intervention (treatment) study, is the treatment procedure well described?

Clearly, with any intervention a sufficient description of the treatment protocol is crucial for the reader to be able to determine whether it seems appropriate to the study hypothesis. For complementary therapies, this question is particularly important as it relates to **ecological validity**. Ecological validity refers to the idea that if a study proposes to evaluate the overall usefulness or safety of a therapy, such as massage or acupuncture, then the treatment used in the study should reflect the way this treatment is used and practised in the real world. Otherwise the study may be assessing the safety or effectiveness of a protocol that does not represent the therapy being studied. If a sham treatment was used for the comparison group, the same issues of validity and appropriateness arise. In other words, for the sham to be valid it must closely resemble the treatment being tested yet not produce the intended treatment effect.

Is treatment randomly assigned, and the method of randomization described?

Just as random selection of participants is necessary to avoid introducing bias, so is random assignment to group. As described in Chapter 4, the best method of randomization is based on the use of a published or computer generated table of random numbers. If the method is not specified or is somehow assumed, the reader should be wary.

Are the outcome measures well described and appropriate given the hypothesis?

Apply common sense again–do the measures used make sense in relation to the study hypothesis? Can you understand them from the description given to the reader? If a measurement tool is relatively new or unfamiliar, such as a newly developed personality inventory for example, the authors should provide information on its reliability and validity, and how these were determined.

Often, reliability is determined based on administering the instrument two or more times and comparing the results to see if they are reasonably similar, or correlated. This method is called **test-retest reliability**, and the higher the correlation (expressed as a percent, such as .87) the better. Validity is commonly estimated by administering the new instrument along with a more established one that measures the same concept or attribute, and again comparing the results to see if they are alike. These procedures and their statistical results should be described.

Are the methods used in calculating both descriptive and inferential statistical analysis described?

Descriptive statistics present the study results (or data set) without generalizing them to a larger group. They simply present the characteristics of the data–such as the difference between the highest and lowest values or the number of categories of response–summarized as the average values for each variable, and the amount of variation of the data around the average.

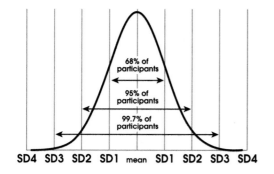

SD4   SD3   SD2   SD1   mean   SD1   SD2   SD3   SD4

Figure 5.1 The Normal Distribution

In statistical terminology, the difference between highest and lowest values is the **range**, the average is referred to as the **mean**, and the degree to which individual results vary around the mean is the **standard deviation (SD)**. The calculation of descriptive statistics is usually straightforward. Some authors may also include information regarding the distribution of the data, that is, whether a line graph of the entire data set would look like a bell-shaped curve. This shape, with most of the scores in the middle and a few on either end, is known as the normal distribution. Figure 5.1 indicates the number of scores that fall within each standard deviation of a normal distribution curve. Many inferential tests are based on the assumption that the data are distributed normally. If this assumption is not true, then the use of some inferential statistical tests may be ruled out.

Inferential statistics are used to draw conclusions about observed differences between groups, and whether these differences can be extrapolated to a larger population. Most inferential statistical tests are designed to determine **statistical significance**, that is, whether the results represent a meaningful result or are due to chance alone. Tests of statistical significance can also estimate the strength of an association between two variables or among a group of variables. Tests that perform this function are useful because they provide an estimated measure of just how much of an outcome is due to the treatment(s) being tested.*

The choice of which type of test is used is partly dependent on the level of data involved. The t-test is an example of a test that requires interval level data, whereas the chi square test (χ^2) can be used with categorical data. Figure 5.2 contains examples of both data types. The subjects' age and education are interval level data, while information related to smoking is categorical. The key difference between the two is that interval data can be plotted on a scale, while with categorical data all subjects fall under one heading or the other.

Participants (n=46)	Means (±SDs)	Range
Age	41.7 (3.2)	18-75
Years of Education	14.5 (2.2)	10-20⁺
Smokers 20		
Non-smokers 26		

Figure 5.2 Levels of Data

The methods used in any inferential statistical analysis should make sense in relation to the study hypothesis and the number of outcome measures (dependent variables). While it is useful to understand the underlying logic of common statistical tests, most beginning readers do not; the important question is whether any tests of statisical significance were performed.

A commonly used measure of both significance and the strength of an association is analysis of variance (ANOVA), because a great deal of information about relationships among the exposures (independent variables) and how these affect the outcome measure can be examined. A related technique, called analysis of covariance (ANCOVA), is sometimes used to factor out the influence of demographic variables when these are unequally distributed between groups prior to treatment,

---

* *In technical language, what percentage of the variance can be attributed to the independent variable.*

to make the groups comparable. For example, imagine a study where two groups were used to assess the effect of exercise on blood pressure, and through attrition one group was younger than the other by the end of the study. To make the two groups comparable again, age might be used as a factor (covariant) in an analysis to remove its confounding effect on blood pressure.

More sophisticated tests using multivariate analysis should be employed when multiple outcomes, which are usually correlated to one another to some extent, are being measured. Multivariate analysis controls for the problem of multiple comparisons among the same group of variables, meaning that if you run enough tests the odds are that one or more of them will appear to be statistically significant when they are really not. The most common method is multiple analysis of variance (MANOVA), used when there are more than two groups being compared across multiple outcome measures. Another method is Hotelling's T^2, used for only two groups.

The key issue is that the authors should present some rationale for the use of the particular statistical procedures chosen, and that these should normally be specified in advance. A complete description of the numerous statistical tests available and their proper use is beyond the scope of this chapter; indeed it would be a book in itself. Fortunately, for those readers who are interested in learning more, such a book does exist. *PDQ Statistics*, by Geoffrey Norman and David Greiner[1], is a concise, well-written, and often humorous guide to statistical tests, with explanations of their proper uses and how to spot their misuse.

Authors may also present the results of a power analysis, which is used to determine how many participants were needed to have at least an 80% chance of finding statistical significance. While this calculation is normally part of the planning stage of a study, some authors choose to report it as a way to justify the sample size chosen. As a guideline regarding sample size, there should be at least 10 participants per outcome measure to have adequate power.[1] Any comparisons between groups that were specified in advance of the data collection may also be presented, as well as the level of statistical significance that will be accepted. The conventional level is .05, or five out of a hundred.

Finally, because computers are almost invariably used now to actually crunch the raw numbers, it is common practice to mention not only the statistical tests used but also the specific software package used to compute them.

Results

Reading the results table in a journal article for the first time is usually an intimidating experience for anyone who is not already comfortable with grasping quantitative information presented in visual form. One way to demystify tables and graphs is to think of them as a type of executive summary presented in a specific kind of shorthand. Breaking down the process into pieces and knowing what questions to ask helps.

As you look at any table of results, the first question to ask is:

Are the tables and graphs clearly labeled?

Identify the demographic results and the inferential results; these will typically be presented in separate tables. Look carefully at the demographic data to determine whether any groups that are being compared to each other are closely matched in terms of factors that could influence the dependent variables or outcomes. In looking at the inferential results, distinguish the treatment or independent variables from the outcome or dependent variables.

Are all the participants accounted for?

Look back to the abstract or methods section for the total number of participants who were enrolled in the study. Check to see if that number matches the sample size listed in the results table, usually abbreviated as n, signifying the number of participants included in the statistical analysis. If the numbers do not match, are the participants who dropped out of the study taken into account in some way? People may choose to leave a study for many different reasons—they leave the area, their life circumstances change, the treatment is unpleasant, or the record-keeping is too time consuming. Regardless of the reasons for drop-out, the risk is that the results may be skewed such that the study may over or underestimate the effect of treatment.

Are means and standard deviations provided?

This information, as part of the descriptive statistical analysis, is usually presented at the beginning of this section's table, or in a separate table if there is more extensive information to warrant it. Because the descriptive analysis is the summary of the raw data before the authors manipulate it, you should view with suspicion any article that fails to list means and standard deviations. Means are usually expressed as a number next to the standard deviations (SD) in parentheses with a plus or minus sign. It typically looks something like this: 45.1 (± 3.46). In this example, 45.1 is the mean, plus or minus a standard deviation of 3.46. It is useful to look at these because large standard deviations mean that there is a great deal of individual variation around the mean. When standard deviations are small, it may indicate a stronger or more consistent treatment effect.

What results of statistical analyses are provided?

The methods section should describe the plan for the statistical analysis, made in advance of the actual collection of the data during the design phase of the study. Depending on the method of analysis, some final statistic such as a t or χ^2 value is arrived at, and the value of this number determines whether or not statistical significance has been reached. You will often see a column labeled DF, which stands for degrees of freedom. The DF is used to calculate the final statistic, and is related to the sample size or n.

Next to these two numbers you will generally see a column labeled p. The value of p indicates the probability that the statistic is due to chance. The smaller the number, the better. The generally accepted standard for p is .05 or less, meaning that the odds of these results occurring from chance alone is smaller than or equal to 5 in 100, or five percent. A p value of .001 means the probability is no more than 1 in 1000. The .05 limit is an arbitrary convention that has become entrenched in most health care literature, although researchers are free to specify in advance what limit of p will be accepted. For example, in a pilot study with a small sample size, the investigators may decide that a p value of .10 will be adequate. In a study with multiple outcomes, investigators may choose to set the p value at .01 to take into account the multiple comparisons among the outcome variables. Although using a multivariate analysis such as MANOVA would be more appropriate, this technique is still considered permissible.

The value of p is often the first thing readers look at in a results table. However, p only indicates whether or not results are due to chance, and is highly sensitive to sample size. With a sufficiently large sample, it is easy to reach statistical significance. A more useful measure of clinical relevance is the effect size, which is a direct indication of how effective a particular treatment is. While methodologists have been stressing the importance of reporting effect sizes for many years, it is still relatively rare for researchers to report them, with the exception of systematic reviews.

The final question to ask in this section is:

Are all the research outcomes reported?

If the authors include a number of outcome measures but show data only for those outcomes that favor or support their hypothesis, the results are suspect. Most peer-reviewed journals would refuse to publish an article with selective reporting of results.

Now that you have a stronger foundation from which to read this section, take a second look at the results section of the Eisenberg article. It is an excellent example of outcomes reporting.

Discussion or Conclusions

Having sorted through the tables, graphs, and charts in the results section, you are ready to read the authors' interpretation of what the numbers mean. The first question to ask in this section is:

Are the authors' comments justified based on the results, and do they follow logically from the results?

Are the conclusions consistent with the data presented, or do the authors go out on a limb making statements that are only tenuously or not at all supported by the data? Do the conclusions make sense in light of the results reported? Another question is:

Do the authors identify weaknesses or limitations in the study design and statistical analysis?

As we discussed in Chapter 3, flaws can be found in any study, no matter how well designed and executed it is. A trustworthy and thoughtful discussion will openly admit the potential biases and limits of the study so that readers can make up their own minds about how much weight to give these. Authors may even suggest ways that future studies might improve upon theirs. Looking back at the Eisenberg study, the authors stress that the results are limited in several respects, in particular by the small number of minority respondents, and they emphasize that the survey results should not be generalized to those populations. This is a fairly good example of such a discussion.

The next question is related to the previous issue of statistical significance:

Is the clinical significance of the study discussed?

As previously mentioned, a large sample size practically guarantees that statistical significance will be reached. However, this does not mean that the results are clinically useful or meaningful. For example, a new drug is demonstrated to reduce the amount of time that patients are deprived of oxygen to the brain following a stroke by an average of five seconds. With a large enough sample size, the p value could be less than .001. Certainly, these results are not due to chance. But will a five second reduction make a clinically significant difference in the survival rate or prognosis for long-term recovery in most patients?

Are the conclusions consistent with the study objectives?

How do the authors relate their results to the study objectives and hypotheses? Have they done what they set out to do in terms of answering their research question? What degree of uncertainty has been reduced by the current study? Related to all of the above is this question:

Would I change the way I practice based on this study?

A primary goal of clinical research is to improve the quality and delivery of health care. The major measure of a study is its imact on clinical practice. In most cases, study results pertain directly to treatment decisions, but not always. In the example of the Eisenberg study, the question might become: Would I change the way I market my services?

References

In looking over the reference list, ask yourself:

How up-to-date and adequate is the reference list?

Check the publication dates, and whether the titles of the references cited seem relevant to the study.

Did the authors examine other articles focusing on similar designs,
population, and outcomes?

Again, the titles of the citations are a good clue. As you become familiar with the literature in your areas of interest, you will also have a better sense of how well the authors have accomplished both these tasks.

Summary

The goal of this chapter has been to introduce a way of thinking about the quality of an article, and to provide some tools to begin breaking down the process of critical thinking into manageable steps. The questions listed here are generally useful, but each one may not always apply to every type of article you may encounter. For example, a case study should not be measured with the same yardstick as a clinical trial. Use your judgement, experience, and common sense.

Critically evaluating a journal article is also a skill that develops with practice. Having come this far, you now have a better understanding of the scientific method and how it is applied in the clinical research setting, as well as some specific guidelines for critiquing an article. The primary objective is to be reasonably skeptical as you read, and to always ask yourself whether some other explanation is possible. The bottom line for any study is this:

How credible is it?

Reference

1. Norman GR, Streiner DL. *PDQ Statistics*. Toronto: B.C. Decker Inc; 1986.

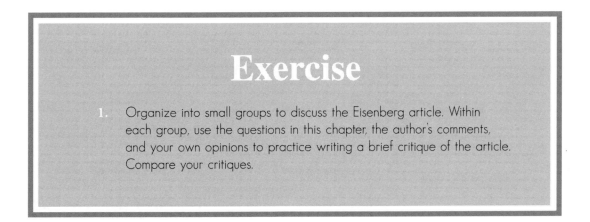

Exercise

1. Organize into small groups to discuss the Eisenberg article. Within each group, use the questions in this chapter, the author's comments, and your own opinions to practice writing a brief critique of the article. Compare your critiques.

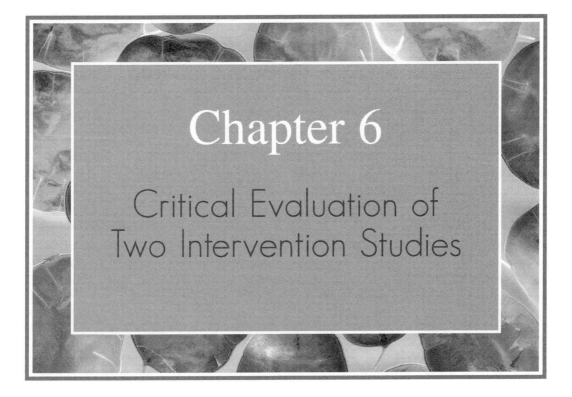

Chapter 6

Critical Evaluation of Two Intervention Studies

Thus the day-to-day business of science consists not in hunting for facts but in testing hypotheses—that is, ascertaining if they or their logical implications are statements about real life or, if inventions, to see whether or not they work.

P. B. Medawar

Learning Objectives

- Identify the three alternative explanations that need to be ruled out in any study.

- Discuss how the clinical significance of a study is evaluated.

- Practice critical evaluation skills.

- Apply research results to your practice.

In this chapter, we will critically evaluate two quantitative articles using as a guide the question and answer format set out in Chapter 5. The subject of the first article is using massage to reduce pain among hospitalized patients who have cancer. The second is a report of a randomized controlled trial of reflexology for women who suffer from premenstrual syndrome (PMS). It is advisable to do a quick read of each article, just to get a sense of the article, and then to go back and read each section in detail, answering the critique questions by yourself or in a discussion group. It is better to avoid reading author comments until after you have completed your own critique.

The approach presented in Chapter 5 and in this chapter is suited to the evaluation of experimental or intervention studies, especially clinical trials. Other types of designs such as case studies or meta-analyses will have other concerns, as discussed previously. As you evaluate quantitative studies, keep in mind that flaws in a study may be due to challenges faced by the researcher(s), who may have encountered logistical problems, technical difficulties, or ethical considerations that could not have been anticipated or reasonably avoided. Try to take a balanced perspective. Almost any study contains flaws; the crucial questions are whether these allow chance, bias, or confounding to be plausible explanations for the study findings, and whether the authors are aware of and discuss the flaws.

Study Example #1: Massage and Cancer Pain

The Effect of Massage on Pain in Cancer Patients

Sally P. Weinrich, PhD, RN: Associate Professor, College of Nursing, University of South Carolina;
Martin C. Weinrich, PhD: Associate Professor, Department of Epidemiology and Biostatistics,
School of Public Health, University of South Carolina, Columbia, SC.

From the College of Nursing and the Department of Epidemiology and Biostatistics,
School of Public Health, University of South Carolina, Columbia, SC.

Address reprint requests to Sally P. Weinrich, PhD, RN. College of Nursing,
University of South Carolina, Columbia, SC 29208.

Applied Nursing Research, Vol. 3, No. 4 (November), 1990: pp.140-145.
©1990 by W.B. Saunders Company.

Abstract: *Evaluating the effectiveness of nursing interventions in decreasing pain is a top priority for clinical research. Unfortunately, most of the research on cancer pain relief has been limited to treatment studies involving the administration of analgesics. Research is needed to determine which nonanalgesic methods of pain control are effective and under what conditions. Consequently, an experimental study was designed to test the effectiveness of massage as an intervention for cancer pain. Twenty-eight patients were randomly assigned to a massage or control group. The patients in the massage group were given a 10 minute massage to the back; the patients in the control group were visited for 10 minutes. For males, there was a significant decrease in pain level immediately after the massage. For females, there was not a significant decrease in pain level immediately after the massage.*

There were no significant differences between pain 1 hour and 2 hours after the massage in comparison with the initial pain for males or females. Massage was shown to be an effective short-term nursing intervention for pain in males in this sample.

Introduction: *Cancer pain remains a frequent and neglected health problem. Thus, proper control of cancer pain is one of the most important issues in the field of oncology (Benedetti & Bonica, 1984; Pritchard, 1988). Dennis, Howes, and Zelanska (1989) found that 715 nurses identified evaluating the effectiveness of nursing interventions in decreasing pain as one of the top priorities for clinical research. Likewise, 85% of an international sample of 669 nurses believed that more emphasis should be given to the management of cancer pain (Pritchard, 1988).*

Every year, approximately 780,000 Americans experience moderate to severe pain due to cancer or cancer therapy (Benedetti & Bonica, 1984). Bonica (1985) estimates that 20% to 40% of cancer pain is inadequately managed. Of Pritchard's (1988) international sample of 669 nurses, 15% believed that cancer patients in their units were given no relief from cancer pain. In a study by Donovan and Dillon (1987) involving 96 patients, only 43% of the patients recalled a nurse discussing anything about their pain with them. Most of the research on cancer pain relief has been limited to treatment studies involving the administration of analgesics (Dalton, Toomey, & Workman, 1988). There is a gap in the literature concerning methods of treatment other than medication for cancer pain.

Current nursing practice needs to consider nonanalgesic methods of pain control as useful adjuncts to pharmacologic therapy of individual patients (Barbour, McGuire, & Kirchhoff, 1986; Daake & Gueldner, 1989; Dalton et al., 1988; Donovan & Dillon, 1987). Pain intensity has been reported to be reduced by a wide range of behaviors including massage, verbalizations, heat and cold application, position changes, distraction, strenuous activity, movement restriction, breathing exercises, hypnosis, relaxation, biofeedback, and guided imagery (Barbour et al., 1986; Wilke, Lovejoy, Dodd, & Tesler, 1988).

Research is needed to determine if and under what specific conditions massage is therapeutic. Massage is thought to be very relaxing and to greatly increase a feeling of well-being (Glaus, 1988). In addition to these benefits, massage is believed to be effective for the relief of pain through the stimulation of the production of endorphins (Tappan, 1988). It is assumed that physiological, mechanical, and reflex effects are accomplished with a 10-minute massage (Tappan, 1988). Dalton et al. (1988) found in their study that the use of massage brought "moderate" and "quite a lot of relief" for 3 of the 5 subjects. Similarly, Barbour et al. (1986) found that massage was reported to decrease pain by 75% in 58 outpatient cancer patients. This pilot study was conducted to confirm the reported effect of massage on pain for cancer patients.

The conceptual framework for this research was the gate control theory of pain (Melzack & Wall, 1982), which includes both sensory and emotional components for pain perception (McGuire, 1987). According to this theory, pain that arises as a result of noxious stimulation (such as cancer pain) may be decreased or increased in its passage from peripheral nerve fibers to those in the spinal cord by the action of a specialized gating mechanism situated in the region of the dorsal horns of the cord (Daake & Gueldner, 1989). The gating mechanism's impact is in modulating sensory input before pain perception and response occur (Barbour et al., 1986). Techniques such as massage, manipulation, relaxation, heat, and ice packs close the gate to the central nervous system (Barbour et al., 1986), resulting in a decrease in pain. Conversely, central activities such as anxiety, excitement, and anticipation may open the gate, resulting in an increase in pain (Daake & Gueldner, 1989).

Method

Research Question: *The purpose of this pilot study was to measure the effect of massage on pain for cancer patients. It was hypothesized that cancer patients who received a 10-minute massage would experience significantly less pain than cancer patients who did not receive a massage.*

Subjects: *Patients were randomly selected from a 30-bed oncology floor of a private hospital in the southeastern United States. Patients were paired based on previous frequency of medication for pain, tranquilizer, or antiemetic effect. Frequencies used for pairing were as follows: within 4 hours (n = 2) within the last 4 to 8 hours (n = 0), within the last 9 hours or more (n = 16), or no medication (n = 10). Each pair of patients was randomly assigned to a treatment or control group.*

A total of 28 cancer patients (14 in each group) participated in the research project. No patients dropped out of the study after they consented to participate. The sample consisted of 18 males and 10 females, 22 whites and 6 blacks. The age range was 36 to 78 years with an average age of 61.5 years old. Of the sample, 21 % (n = 6) were receiving radiation; 21% (n = 6), chemotherapy; and 11% (n = 3), a combination of radiation and chemotherapy. Eighteen of the subjects had received medication within the 3-day time period before initiation of the study. Seven of the subjects received medication within 4 hours before the intervention, and 7 of the subjects received medication within the 2-hour time period after the intervention.

Instrument: *A Visual Analogue Scale (VAS) (Figure 1) was used to measure the self-report of pain intensity (McGuire, 1988). The scale consists of a 10-mm line with end points of* no pain *and* pain as bad as it could possibly be.

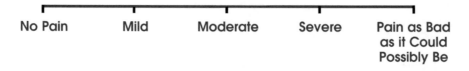

Figure 1. Visual Analogue Scale.

Each patient was asked to place a mark through the line at the point that best described how much pain he or she was experiencing at that particular moment. The point on the line is measured and used as the score. The VAS assumes equal intervals for scoring. The VAS has been shown to be a reliable and sensitive measure of the patient's subjective experience of pain (Chapman et al., 1985; Ohnhaus & Adler, 1975; Syrjala & Chapman, 1984). Price, McGrath, & Rafii (1983) have validated the use of the VAS in chronic and experimental pain. Revill, Robinson, & Rosen (1976) demonstrated that the VAS was reliable on repeated measurements ($r = 0.95$, $p < .001$). Cronbach alpha reliability for this study was 97.*

Procedure: *A 1-hour training session on massage technique, interviewing procedure, and the use of the VAS was provided to the data collectors before the research project began. Seven senior nursing students conducted the intervention activities for the paired groups. All of the interviews and interventions (massage or control) were carried out between 9 a.m. and 12 noon. The massage and interviewing procedures of each student were validated at the completion of both days of the study.*

Initially, each patient was asked to indicate the current level of pain on the VAS. For the treatment group, the patient was given a 10-minute Swedish massage to the back by the data collector. The back was massaged in a slow, continuous, upward manner with the use of lotion. The muscles of the back provided the direction for the massage. For the control group, no physical contact was initiated, and the data collector sat and visited with the patient for 10 minutes. The control was intended to account for the possible non-specific effects of the data collector's time and effort with patients. For both the control and treatment groups, data collectors were instructed to respond as they usually would to verbal comments of patients. Immediately after the procedure, patients in both the control and treatment groups were asked to indicate their level of pain. Self-reported levels of pain were collected again 1 and 2 hours after the intervention. Data on medication taken during the time of the study was retrieved from patient charts after the last self-reported pain level was obtained.

Findings

On a VAS scale of 0 to 10, self-reported pain levels before the procedure ranged from 0 to 9, with a mean of 2.6. Subjects in the treatment group had higher levels of initial pain ($M = 3.1$) than subjects in the control group ($M = 2.2$). Gender difference existed in the level of pain, with males in the treatment group having the highest levels of pain ($M = 4.19$) (Table 1). Mean pain levels immediately after the procedure, 1 hour after the procedure, and 2 hours after the procedure are shown in Figure 2.

Analysis of covariance and repeated measures were performed to detect group differences in perceived pain over time. The VAS level of pain before the procedure was the covariate

---

* r, called the correlation coefficient, is a measure of how closely one measure corresponds to another measure, like weighing yourself several times on the same scale on the same day, and seeing how close the scores are. The higher the value of r, the more closely correlated the measures are to one another. Correlation is often used to show the degree of relationship between variables

Time of Measurement	Treatment Group			Control Group			Total
	Males	Females	Both	Males	Females	Both	
Initial	4.19 (2.6)	1.65 (2.7)	3.1 (2.8)	1.93 (2.7)	2.73 (4.2)	2.2 (3.0)	2.6 (2.9)
Immediately after the Procedure	2.93 (2.3)	1.43 (2.3)	2.3 (2.3)	2.06 (2.7)	2.63 (4.3)	2.2 (3.1)	2.3 (2.7)
1 Hour after the Procedure	3.03 (2.1)	1.40 (2.2)	2.3 (2.2)	1.87 (2.6)	2.63 (4.3)	2.1 (3.0)	2.2 (2.6)
2 Hours after the Procedure	2.38 (2.1)	1.40 (2.2)	2.0 (2.1)	1.09 (1.2)	2.35 (4.4)	1.5 (2.4)	1.7 (2.3)

Table 1. Mean (Standard Deviation) Pain Levels on the Visual Analogue Scale

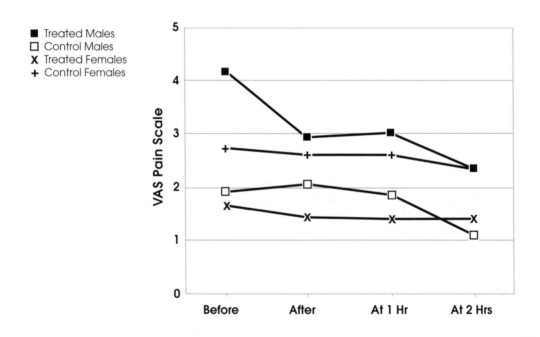

Figure 2. Mean Level of Pain by Gender and Procedure Group

in the analysis of covariance. Repeated measures were used to measure changes in the VAS level of pain immediately after the procedure, 1 hour, and 2 hours after the procedure. Medication taken before the study and medication taken during the study were included in the analyses. Significant differences between gender and massage intervention led to separate analyses for males and females. For males, there was a significant decrease in pain levels immediately after the massages ($F(5,13) = 8.24$, $p = .01$). For females, no significant difference was found after the massage ($F(4,6) = 2.52$, $p = .17$) In the repeated measures analyses, there were no significant differences between pain 1 hour and 2 hours after the massages in comparison with the initial pain for males or females. Age had no significant effect on pain at any of the four VAS measures. For both males and females, there was no significant difference in the control groups.

Evaluating the effect of medicines yielded interesting and surprising results. Medication given 1 and/or 2 hours after the procedure was not significantly associated with a decrease in self-reported pain levels for the sample as a whole ($F(5,23) = 0.36$, $p = .56$), for the pain level at 1 hour after the procedure ($F(5,23) = 1.25$, $p = .28$). and for the pain level 2 hours after the procedure. Medication given 1 to 4 hours before the procedure was not significantly associated with a decrease in pain at the measure of pain taken immediately after the intervention ($F(4,24) = 1.44$, $p = .24$) or 1 hour after the intervention ($F(5,23) = 3.09$, $p = .09$). However, this medication was associated with a decrease in pain 2 hours after the intervention ($F(5,23) = 9.03$, $p = .006$). When the analyses were performed separately for males and females, medications given before the intervention were significant for the females ($F(3,7) = 29.37$, $p = .002$), but not for the males ($F(3,15) = .03$, $p = .87$). In summary, medication was not effective in reducing pain levels for any of the subjects until more than 2 hours after administration of the medication.

Discussion

In this pilot study, pain relief was significantly decreased immediately after a massage for males, but not for females. Although there was a decrease in pain for the males 1 and 2 hours after the massage, it was not significantly different from the decrease in pain for the females or for the control group (males or females). According to this study's conceptual framework, the gate control theory of pain, the massage could have temporarily closed the gate for the males, decreasing the pain.

The low intensity of pain in the control group (males and females) and the females in the experimental group is a limitation of the study. Significance was obtained for the subjects who had high levels of pain (males in the experimental group). Additional research on subjects in high levels of pain is needed to determine whether the benefit of a massage extends to all persons with high levels of pain or applies only to males. Subjects were paired and divided into control or experimental groups based on the variable of frequency of medication before the study. It was assumed that frequency of medication would be related to pain levels with patients who had more pain taking more medication. In this study, the patients who had more pain did not take more medicine. Consequently, the treatment group had higher pain levels than the control group. We recommend that future studies on pain intervention use a self-reported measure of pain as the variable for pairing rather than the frequency of medication, as was done in this study.

Similarly, this study did not use gender as a basis for division into control or treatment group. In this study, males had higher self-reported levels of pain than females. Gender difference in the effect of a massage as well as the effectiveness of medication are apparent in this study and require further research. Also, gender differences in methods of coping with pain need to be explored. Could the males use fewer coping behaviors for pain than the females, resulting in increased effectiveness of the massage? Or perhaps, there is greater social acceptability of massage in the males than in the females.

This pilot study provides support for use of alternative methods of pain alleviation, such as massage in males, simultaneously with medication. The males in this study obtained an immediate decrease in pain levels after the massage. Medication was not effective in reducing pain levels until more than 2 hours after administration of the medication for any of the subjects. Based on the males in this pilot study, massage could be used for immediate pain relief, and medication could be used for long-term (2 hours) pain relief in males. Future research needs to focus on the complementary effect of medication and massage.

The Donovan and Dillon (1987) study showed that nurses usually do not discuss pain with patients. The impact of discussing pain with patients needs to be evaluated. Donovan (1989) has also discovered that the environment in which care is given is important to a patient's pain relief. The effect of the environment needs to be studied, as well as the effect of the provider. For example, would pain alleviation be different for a back rub given by a family member, a primary nurse, a staff nurse, or a student nurse?

References

1. Barbour, L., McGuire, D., & Kirchhoff, K. (1986). Nonanalgesic methods of pain control used by cancer outpatients. Oncology Nursing Forum, 136: 56-60.

2. Benedetti, C., & Bonica. J. (1984). Cancer pain: Basic considerations. In C. Benedetti, C.R., Chapman, G.M. Moricca (Eds.). Recent Advances in the Management of Pain (pp. 71-101). New York, NY: Raven.

3. Bonica, J. (1985). Treatment of cancer pain: Current status and future needs. In H.L. Fields, R. Dubner, & F. Cervero (Eds.), Advances in Pain Research and Therapy, 9: 589-616. New York. NY: Raven.

4. Chapman, C., Casev. K., Dubner. R., Foley, K., Gracely, R.,& Reading, A. (1985). Pain measurement: An overview. Pain, 22: 1-31.

5. Daake. D.R., & Gueldner, S.H. (1989). Imagery instruction and the control of postsurgical pain. Applied Nursing Research, 2: 114-120.

6. Dalton, J., Toomey, T., & Workman, M. (1988). *Pain relief for cancer patients.* Cancer Nursing, *11: 322-328.*

7. Dennis, K., Howes, D., & Zelauskas, B. (1989). *Identifying nursing research priorities: A first step in program development.* Applied Nursing Research, *2: 108-113.*

8. Donovan, M., & Dillon, P. (1987). *Incidence and characteristics of pain in a sample of hospitalized cancer patients.* Cancer Nursing, *10: 85-92.*

9. Donovan, M.I. (1989). *An historical view of pain management: How we got to where we are!* Cancer Nursing, *12: 257-261.*

10. Glaus. A. (1988). *The position of nursing.* Cancer Nursing, *11: 250-253.*

11. McGuire, D. (1987). *The multidimensional phenomenon of cancer pain.* In D.B. McGuire & C.H. Yarbro (Eds.), Cancer Pain Management *(pp. 1-20). Orlando, FL: Grune & Stratton.*

12. McGuire, D. (1988). *Measuring pain.* In M. Frank-Stromborg (Ed.), Instruments for Clinical Nursing Research *(pp. 333-356). Norwalk, CT: Appleton & Lange.*

13. Melzack, R., & Wall, P. (1982). The Challenge of Pain. *New York, NY: Basic Books.*

14. Ohnhaus, E., & Adler, R. (1975). *Methodological problems in the measurement of pain: A comparison between the verbal rating scale and the visual analogue scale.* Pain, *1: 379-384.*

15. Price. D., McGrath, D., & Rafii, A. (1983). *The validation of visual analogue scales as ratio scale measures for chronic and experimental pain.* Pain, *17: 45-46.*

16. Pritchard, A.P. (1988). *Management of pain and nursing attitudes.* Cancer Nursing, *11: 203-209.*

17. Revill, S., Robinson, J., & Rosen, M. (1976). *The reliability of a linear analogue for evaluating pain.* Anaesthesia, *31: 1191-1198.*

18. Svrjala, K., & Chapman, C. (1984). *Measurement of clinical pain: A review and integration of research findings.* In C. Benedetti, C.R. Chapman, G.M. Moricca (Eds.), Recent Advances in the Management of Pain *(pp. 251-264). New York. NY: Raven.*

19. Tappan. F. (1988). Healing Massage Techniques. *Norwalk, CT: Appleton & Lange.*

20. Wilke, D., Lovejoy, N., Dodd, M., & Tesler, M. (1988). *Cancer pain control behaviors: Description and correlation with pain intensity.* Oncology Nursing Forum, *15: 723-731.*

Critical Evaluation Questions

1. What information, if any, is missing from the abstract?

2. Is the study objective clearly stated in the introduction?

3. Are the study's context and relevance clearly established?

4. In the methods section, is the sample well described, including inclusion/exclusion criteria and method of selection?

5. Are blinding procedures used, and if so, how well did they work?

6. Is a comparison or placebo group part of the design?

7. Is the treatment procedure well described and appropriate given the hypothesis?

8. Is treatment randomly assigned, and is the method of randomization described?

9. Are the outcome measures well described and appropriate given the hypothesis?

10. Are the methods used in calculating both descriptive and inferential statistical analysis described?

11. In the results section, are the tables and graphs clearly labeled?

12. Are all the participants accounted for?

13. Are means and standard deviations provided?

14. What results of statistical analyses are provided?

15. Are all the research outcomes previously specified reported?

16. In the discussion section, are the authors' comments justified, based on the results?

17. Do the conclusions follow logically from the results?

18. Do the authors identify weaknesses or limitations in the study design or analysis?

19. Is the clinical significance of the study discussed?

20. Are the conclusions consistent with the study objectives?

21. How up to date and adequate is the reference list?

22. Did the authors examine other articles focusing on similar designs, populations, and outcomes?

23. The last question to consider about an article: Based on the results of this study, would you make any changes in your practice?

Critical Evaluation

Now that you have read through the article once, go back and read each section again, this time attempting to answer the critical evaluation questions.

Remember to be somewhat skeptical as you read. If you can locate a hard copy of the journal, check the guidelines for authors to determine whether the journal sends out its submissions for blind review by other experts in the field, that is, without author information, so that editorial readers are not influenced by author identity or affiliation. If editors or reviewers and their credentials are listed, determine if you can the extent of their expertise about massage (or any other complementary therapy being studied) and other areas of expertise relevant to the study.

• Comments on this Study's Abstract

What information, if any, is missing?

This abstract uses a narrative format rather than the standardized one, so the reader has to work a little harder to pull out the relevant information. The research question is introduced, and the design is described in general terms. The methods are not described in detail, but you can identify the number of subjects, and that the subjects were randomly assigned to either a treatment group who received a 10 minute massage or a control group who were visited for 10 minutes. The results are described in general terms and a conclusion reached. Based on the information in this abstract, the research hypothesis sounds very broad and the methods used to answer it raise questions because they seem inadequate to such a large task. A knowledgeable reader will plan ahead to scrutinize the methods section carefully.

• Comments on the Introduction

Is the study objective clearly stated?

Yes. The authors cite two other studies where massage was used to reduce cancer pain and state that they conducted a pilot study to confirm the reported effects of massage on pain for cancer patients. Note that one of the other studies (Barbour, 1986) was a survey of cancer outpatients—even without familiarity with the Barbour study, you can get a sense of this from the title of the article as listed in the references. However, the specific research question is not stated until the methods section of the article.

Are the study's context and relevance clearly established?

The authors provide a compelling case for the importance of conducting the study in light of the problem of pain related to cancer, and the role that other interventions (in addition to medication) can play. Because massage is reported by cancer patients to be a frequently used method of pain reduction, the authors give a clear rationale that justifies the need for a study evaluating the effects of massage on cancer pain. They also provide the gate control theory of pain as a conceptual framework for their argument.

However, the authors provide a reference (Tappan, 1988) as the basis for their assumption that physiological, mechanical, and reflex effects are accomplished with a 10 minute massage. There is no mention of studies or clinical anecdote to support this assertion in the Tappan edition cited, in either the sections on effects of massage or on massage and pain. And the Barbour survey is used twice to support a statement describing the proposed neurological mechanism of the gating response. From the context, a reader might think the survey was instead a laboratory-based study. A less knowledgeable reader, unfamiliar with the literature, might give more credibility to these statements than is warranted.

Another problem with this article's review of the literature is that an important area of previous research is missing altogether. There is a large body of studies investigating differences between how men and women report their pain and respond to treatments for pain. No mention of these studies or the general issue of gender differences in regard to pain is made in the introduction, and this is a significant lapse.

•   Comments on the Methods Section

Is the sample well described, including inclusion/exclusion criteria and method of selection?

The description of the subjects is sketchy at best, and the method of randomization is not mentioned. Although some demographic data are given for the sample as a whole, no table that describes the demographics of each group for comparison purposes is provided. From the information given it is impossible to determine the male to female ratio, age, and ethnicity in each group. No inclusion/exclusion criteria are given. In terms of selection, subjects were recruited from a 30-bed unit, and 28 of 30 possible patients agreed to participate. In essence, this appears to be a convenience sample drawn from a small private community-based hospital.

Although subjects from each group were matched according to medication for pain, anxiety, and nausea, no information is given regarding the type of cancer, stage of disease, or type of chemotherapy. Therapists who have worked with people with cancer know that different cancers cause varying degrees of discomfort, that the later stages of cancer are more likely to have metastasized to other locations such as the spinal vertebrae, which can cause severe pain, and that some chemotherapy drugs are harder to tolerate than others. It seems likely that the patients in this relatively small sample may not have been truly comparable to one another, in other words, that there was a great deal of individual variation that could have influenced the results.

Are blinding procedures used, and if so, how well did they work?

No blinding procedures are described.

Is a comparison or placebo group part of the design?

Yes. Subjects in the treatment group were compared to those who received a 10-minute conversational visit, in an attempt to control for the nonspecific effects of attention. Little is said about the parameters for the visit, such as whether a script was followed, or whether patients were encouraged to respond to open-ended questions. In addition, the 10-minute visit does not control for the nonspecific effects of touch.

Is the treatment procedure well described and appropriate given the hypothesis?

Yes and no. The authors state that the massage was performed by senior nursing students who received an hour-long training in massage, interviewing procedure, and how to administer the Visual Analogue Scale. Thus, the reader can conclude that the people providing massage received less than an hour of training specifically in how to perform the massage. In addition, the gender of the students is not specified.

From the description, it appears that the massage consisted of 10 minutes of effleurage to the back, following the direction of the back muscles. This standardized protocol is problematic in relation to the research question. An experienced therapist familiar with the needs of people with cancer would tailor the treatment to the individual patient's need, which would likely increase the effectiveness of the intervention. It also seems probable that more than 10 minutes of massage would be needed to produce effective pain reduction in this population.

Is treatment randomly assigned, and is the method of randomization described?

Treatment is stated to have been randomly assigned, but the method of randomization is not described. Subjects were paired, however, based on their use of medication, in an attempt to control for the influence of this variable.

Are the outcome measures well described and appropriate given the hypothesis?

Yes. A clear description, along with background information justifying the use of the Visual Analogue Scale, is included. Data on medication use was taken directly from each patient's chart. Both seem appropriate to the research question.

Are the methods used in calculating both descriptive and inferential statistical analysis described?

Not in the methods section. These are included in the results section instead. The authors used analysis of covariance to control for the higher level of initial pain reported by males in the treatment group. From the authors' description, it is difficult to tell whether plans for statistical analysis were specified in advance, or were based on what the data showed.

Comments on the Results Section

Are the tables and graphs clearly labeled?

Yes, the tables and graphs are straightforward and easy to read. The graph of the Visual Analogue Scale pain data is easier to grasp visually compared to the explanation in the text.

Are all the participants accounted for?

Yes. No patients dropped out of the study after agreeing to participate.

Are means and standard deviations provided?

Yes. Means are given for the demographic data in the text; means and standard deviations are provided for the VAS data in Table 1. Standard deviations are given in parentheses. Notice the relative size of the means and the standard deviations—the SDs are fairly large. This means that there is a large amount of individual variation in the pain scores. A graph showing the change in pain scores over time by group is also given in Figure 2. Values for p, the level of statistical significance, are given in the text.

What results of statistical analyses are provided?

The results of analysis of the VAS data are presented in Table 1 and Figure 2. Some demographic data and the results of an analysis of the medication use along with their p values, and more of the VAS data are all included in the text. The analysis of the medication data is difficult to read—a third table or graph might have made this information easier for readers to grasp. It appears that because of unanticipated differences between males and females in the sample, a separate and additional analysis was performed.

Although values for p are given, the effect size is not reported, nor is a power analysis included to determine whether the sample size was adequate to detect a true difference between groups. Notice too that there is a fairly large initial difference between the treatment and the control group. A possible alternative explanation for the reduction in pain following the treatment could be regression to the mean, a concept explained in Chapter 1.

Are all the research outcomes previously specified reported?

Yes.

Comments on the Discussion Section

Are the authors' comments justified, based on the results?

This is often a difficult question to answer. In this case, the authors speculate that the gate control theory worked only for the males. Does this seem likely to you? It does appear that there are some gender differences in terms of how males and females responded to the massage; however, because the sample was not more homogeneous it is difficult to say whether the differences were due to gender or some other factor. Remember that each group consisted of fourteen patients, and that the number of males relative to females per group is not specified. While we do not know precisely how many males are being compared to how many females in the treatment group, it seems probable that the numbers are quite small. How willing should we be to make a clinical generalization based on such a small sample size?

Do the conclusions follow logically from the results?

Given the problems already discussed in the design of the study, arguably they do not. The ambiguous results seen in this study could be due to flaws in the design that introduced a large amount of individual variation. The methods used are clearly not a good fit for answering such a broad research question. It certainly seems possible that there are plausible alternative explanations for the results; for example, perhaps the males in the study were responding to being massaged by a female nursing student. In addition, ten minutes of effleurage on the back performed by an untrained student is probably not the most effective or even valid method to assess whether massage is helpful in reducing pain for people with various types and stages of cancer.

Do the authors identify weaknesses or limitations in the study design or analysis?

The authors do identify one limitation—the relatively higher pain intensity among males in the treatment group, compared to the females in the treatment group and the entire control group. The authors also discuss their assumptions regarding the spurious relationship between pain levels and medication use, and make some recommendations for future research.

One limitation previously mentioned in our discussion is the lack of any mention regarding pain and gender differences. Another major limitation not discussed by the authors is the lack of understanding of massage as it is clinically practiced. As previously mentioned, a major weakness in this study is the operational definition of massage, which was ill suited to provide effective pain relief for the participants.

Finally, the sample size is small for the number of statistical analyses that were performed. A careful reader would wonder whether there was sufficient power to detect a true treatment effect. The large reduction in pain seen among males in the study may have been the result of statistical error—too many tests performed on too little data, with a large amount of individual variation mixed in. This is another reason why unusual findings often require replication in order to be considered credible.

Is the clinical significance of the study discussed?

Some recommendations for the use of massage in addition to medication are made. However, based on these results, would you as a hospital administrator decide to immediately implement a program of massage? It would appear that the results support providing massage for male patients with cancer but not females, a type of decision-making that requires stronger evidence than this study presents.

Because the study measures pain, the question also arises: what degree of pain reduction is clinically meaningful? There must be a standard defined by the authors or that makes sense to the reader, and this is not provided. For example, the authors could give the percentage of patients who experienced a reduction in pain, or the extent of pain reduction, as demonstrated by visual analogue scale scores.

Are the conclusions consistent with the study objectives?

In general, this study raises more questions than it answers, as do the authors in the discussion section. Based on the small sample size, lack of fit between the overly broad research question and the methods used to answer it, and other possible explanations for the statistical results, it is difficult to place a high degree of confidence in the findings. Surprisingly, given that this is not a study that strongly supports the use of massage for reducing cancer pain, it is still frequently cited as a supporting reference in the literature reviews of more recent studies.

•   Comments on the Reference List

How up to date and adequate is the reference list?

The reference list seems adequate and up to date given the publication date of the article.

Did the authors examine other articles focusing on similar designs, populations, and outcomes?

Certainly the authors considered other studies on pain in cancer patients. Given the paucity of research on massage at the time when this study was planned, conducted, and published, it is not surprising that other contemporary studies on massage are not cited—hardly any existed.

Based on the results of this study, would you make any changes in your practice?

Probably not. The flaws in this study and the ambiguous nature of the results make it difficult to have a high degree of confidence in it. It seems as likely that chance and error could explain these findings as the explanation put forward by the authors.

Study Example #2: Reflexology and PMS

Randomized Controlled Study of Premenstrual Symptoms Treated With Ear, Hand, and Foot Reflexology

Terry Oleson, PhD and William Flocco

From the Division of Behavioral Medicine, California Graduate Institute, Los Angeles; and the American Academy of Reflexology, Burbank, California. This study was funded by private contributions to the California Graduate Institute and the American Academy of Reflexology.

Address reprint requests to: Terry Oleson, PhD, Division of Behavioral Medicine, California Graduate Institute, 1100 Glendon Avenue, Suite 1118, Los Angeles, CA 90024

Received November 19,1992. Received in revised form June 30, 1993. Accepted July 7,1993.

Abstract

Objective: To determine whether reflexology therapy—the application of manual pressure to reflex points on the ears, hands, and feet that somatotopically correspond to specific areas of the body—can significantly reduce premenstrual symptoms compared to placebo treatment.

Methods: Thirty-five women who complained of previous distress with premenstrual syndrome (PMS) were randomly assigned to be treated by ear, hand, and foot reflexology or to receive placebo reflexology. All subjects completed a daily diary, which monitored 38 premenstrual symptoms on a four-point scale. Somatic and psychological indicators of premenstrual distress were recorded each day for 2 months before treatment, for 2 months during reflexology, and for 2 months afterward. The reflexology sessions for both groups were provided by a trained reflexology therapist once a week for 8 weeks, and lasted 30 minutes each.

Results: Analysis of variance for repeated measures demonstrated a significantly greater decrease in premenstrual symptoms for the women given true reflexology treatment than for the women in the placebo group.

Conclusion: These clinical findings support the use of ear, hand, and foot reflexology for the treatment of PMS. (Obstet Gynecol 1993; 82:906-11)

Introduction

In 1931, Frank[1] observed that many women suffer varying degrees of discomfort in the days preceding the onset of menstruation. Nader[2] found that most subsequent studies estimated the prevalence of premenstrual syndrome (PMS) at 30-40%. One survey[3] of 1826 women reported that 85% of the respondents complained of one or more premenstrual symptoms. Nonetheless, the etiology and treatment of PMS remain controversial. Because the physical and psychological symptoms reported by women are most severe during the late luteal phase of the menstrual cycle, one proposed mechanism for PMS has been related to progesterone levels. However, several controlled studies have failed to find progesterone administration to be more effective than placebo. A randomized, controlled, double-blind, crossover study of 168 women showed that progesterone suppositories did reduce premenstrual symptoms, but this decrease was not significantly greater than with placebo administration.[4] In a 1-year follow-up of these women,[5] only 27% of the original subjects were still taking the progesterone medications, and there was no significant difference in premenstrual symptoms between women taking and those not taking progesterone.

Other double-blind, randomized, placebo-controlled studies of PMS treatment have examined various gonadotropin-releasing hormone agonists[6,7] and different oral contraceptives.[8,9] In each of these investigations, the active medications were shown to alleviate some of the physical symptoms of PMS significantly more than placebos, but less consistent results were found for the mood changes that often precede menstrual flow. Conversely, placebo-controlled studies of anxiolytic[10,11] and antidepressant[12-14] medications have shown significant improvement in mood-related premenstrual symptoms compared to the effects of placebo medications, but less pronounced results with somatic symptoms.

A different approach to the treatment of PMS has been reduction of stress by procedures other than psychotropic medications. Goodale et al[15] demonstrated significantly greater alleviation of premenstrual symptoms in women trained to produce Benson's relaxation response than in women who participated in a reading control group or in women who just charted their symptoms. The degree of improvement was highest for women with the most severe PMS.

The present study sought to investigate whether reflexology therapy can reduce premenstrual distress. Reflexology involves the manual stimulation of reflex points on the ears, hands, and feet that correspond somatotopically to specific areas and organs of the body. In his review of the reflexology literature, Dale[16] noted the occurrence of several "cutaneo-organ reflex points" on the foot, which were first described by Fitzgerald in 1917. Dale further delineated the microacupuncture reflex systems found on the ears, hands, feet, nose, tongue, and teeth, which are "holographic reiterations of the anatomy of the body." Although acupuncture points on the auricle were known by ancient Chinese physicians, Nogier first described the inverted fetus topology of reflex points represented on the external ear in 1957.[17] Oleson et al[18] conducted a double-blind evaluation of these auricular points to demonstrate the diagnostic validity of the somatotopic representation of particular parts of the body at specific ear reflex points. The present investigation is believed to be the first placebo-controlled trial of the effect of reflexology treatment on any clinical condition.

Materials and Methods

From October 1988 to November 1990, women reporting premenstrual symptoms were recruited using newspaper advertisements and were then given a telephone interview. After all research procedures were presented, subjects who agreed to participate were required to give written informed consent. Potential participants were disqualified if they were pregnant, reported a serious physical or psychiatric illness, had extensive prior experience with reflexology, or were taking estrogen or progesterone specifically for PMS. All subjects were interviewed by a clinical psychologist to exclude individuals with severe psychological disturbance.

Each subject was asked to keep a daily record of PMS symptoms, consisting of 19 somatic symptoms such as sensations of breast tenderness, abdominal bloating, and menstrual cramps, and 19 psychological symptoms, including feeling anxious, depressed, irritated, and critical. These items were selected from several previous research questionnaires on PMS.[4,6,10] The daily diary also provided a space for the women to indicate when they experienced their monthly menstrual flow. Subjects rated each symptom on a four-point rating scale[19] using the following values: 0 (none), 1 (mild), 2 (moderate), and 3 (strong). The premenstrual score for each symptom was the sum of the symptom scores for the 7 days before menstruation, a time period used in several previous studies.[4,8,10] A 7-day symptom score on the 0-3 scale could range between 0-21. Although for most items a high score indicated severe premenstrual distress, three measures of positive mood—feelings of well-being, energy, and excitement or alertness—were scored in the reverse direction and their value subtracted from 21.

Somatic, psychological, and total symptom scores were obtained by deriving the sum of the daily scores for the 7 days before the onset of menses and computing the mean value across all items. Alpha coefficients for these three principal measures indicated high internal consistency during the baseline charting period: 0.92 for the total PMS scale, 0.82 for the somatic symptoms scale, and 0.94 for the psychological symptoms scale. Comparing the first two menstrual periods for all subjects, there was high test-retest reliability for the total PMS scale ($r = 0.87$), and these premenstrual scores were highly correlated to the Health Distress Index ($r = 0.62$). A separate study of 12 untreated women who were asked to complete the same daily PMS diary revealed that these premenstrual distress scores remained stable over time for 6 consecutive months ($F = 2.26$, $P > .1$, one-way repeated-measures analysis of variance).

After they had recorded premenstrual symptoms each day for at least two menstrual cycles before the first treatment, all participants were randomly assigned, using a random numbers table, to either the true reflexology group or the placebo group according to the order of their first reflexology session appointment.[20] The subjects were informed that they would receive one of two types of reflexology therapy, each of which had the potential to relieve premenstrual symptoms. They did not know which treatment they received. The subjects continued the daily charting for 2 more months while receiving weekly reflexology sessions and then for another 2 months after treatment.

Participants in both the true and placebo reflexology groups attended 30-minute, individual reflexology sessions once a week for 8 weeks. The subjects lay supine on a treatment table while one of several trained reflexology therapists touched specific areas of *their ears, hands, and feet. True reflexology therapy consisted of manual pressure to the areas of the ears, hands, and feet that correspond to specific areas of the body. The reflex points considered appropriate for the treatment of PMS include points on the hands and feet for the ovary, uterus, pituitary gland, adrenal gland, kidney, celiac or solar plexus, and sympathetic nervous system.[16] In addition to these regions, manual pressure to the ear was also applied to the Chinese auricular reflex point shen men,[17] and the Chinese acupuncture point on the hand known as* hoku *or large intestine 4.[16] Figure 1 illustrates the precise locations of these reflex points on the ears, hands, and feet. Appropriate reflex points tend to be more sensitive to applied pressure than the surrounding tissue, and thus they were manipulated firmly yet soothingly.*

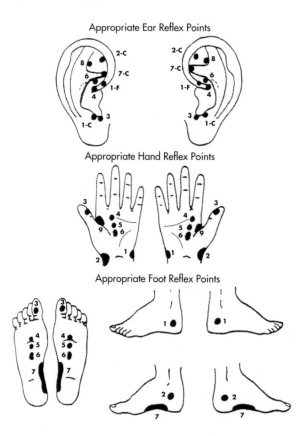

Figure 1. Location of appropriate ear, hand, and foot reflex points[16] where manual pressure was applied to participants in the true reflexology group. Numbers indicate the part of the body to which that reflex point somatotopically corresponds: 1 = ovary; 2 = uterus; 3 = pituitary gland and endocrine system; 4 = solar plexus (point zero on the ear); 5 = adrenal gland; 6 = kidney; 7 = sympathetic nervous system; 8 = Chinese ear point *shen men*; 9 = Chinese meridian point *hoku* or large intestine 4. Where there is a difference in the location of auricular points between Chinese and French charts,[17] the Chinese representation is indicated by the extension "C"; the French representation is indicated by the extension "F".

Subjects in the placebo reflexology group were given uneven tactile stimulation to areas of the ears, hands, and feet not considered appropriate for the treatment of PMS. The reflex points considered inappropriate for menstrual problems included the nose, ear, shoulder, upper arm, elbow, abdomen, and mouth. The different locations of these placebo reflex points are shown in Figure 2. Manual pressure applied in the placebo treatment was either overly light or very rough. Nonetheless, every effort was made to make the placebo reflexology sessions appear similar to the true reflexology treatment with regard to the manner in which the therapy was provided. During these sessions, all placebo subjects reported that they found the treatment relaxing and pleasant, although a few participants did complain that the manual pressure was sometimes too light. All subjects indicated that they felt they were receiving actual reflexology therapy.

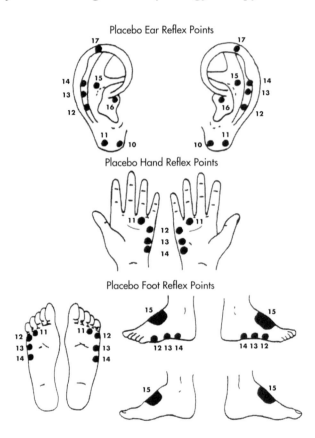

Figure 2. Location of inappropriate ear, hand, and foot reflex points where manual pressure was applied to participants in the placebo reflexology group. Numbers indicate the part of the body to which that reflex point somatotopically conesponds: 10 = nose; 11 = ear; 12 = shoulder; 13 = upper arm; 14 = elbow; 15 = abdomen; 16 = mouth; 17 = helix point represented on Chinese ear charts.

The mean of the first two premenstrual periods recorded during the baseline charting period was compared to the mean of the two premenstrual periods examined during the 8 weeks of reflexology sessions and the mean of the two premenstrual periods following treatment. Statistical differences between the true reflexology and placebo reflexology groups were analyzed by two-way analysis of variance with repeated measures, using as independent factors the type of treatment and the PMS charting period. In addition, a percent decrease in PMS was obtained by dividing the difference between the baseline and treatment periods by the baseline period.

Results

All subjects who passed the initial telephone screening were sent packets of demographic questionnaires and several copies of the premenstrual symptoms diary. Thirty-three of the 83 women who began daily charting of PMS symptoms failed to complete the first 2 months of baseline measurements. Further attrition occurred after the subjects were randomly assigned to one of the two treatment groups; seven participants in the true reflexology group and eight in the placebo reflexology group dropped out of the study for various reasons. The high attrition rate is not surprising in a study with such a long evaluation phase and treatment period, despite our efforts to keep all volunteers in the study. The mean age of the 35 women in the two treatment groups was 35.6 years, ranging from 24-47. Most of the women were white (83%), single (57%), and childless (66%), had some college or had received a Bachelor's degree (69%), and earned an annual income of $16,000-40,000 (69%). Table 1 shows the demographic variables for each treatment group. The diagnosis of PMS was considered appropriate if the mean total score in the premenstrual phase was at least twice that for the week after menstruation. All participants fulfilled this criterion, exhibiting a progressive rise in premenstrual symptoms 3-10 days before the onset of menstrual flow and a pronounced decrease in these symptoms on the third or fourth day after menstruation began.

Table 2 shows the mean and standard deviation (SD) for the total PMS scale, somatic symptoms scale, and psychological symptoms scale for the true reflexology and placebo reflexology groups for the three time periods. For each of these three measures, premenstrual scores were similar for the two groups during baseline charting, showed greater reduction for the true reflexology group during the treatment period, and rose only slightly for each group during the post-treatment period. Two-way analysis of variance for repeated measures revealed a significant interaction between treatment groups and times of measurement. Statistical analyses of the interaction effect showed that treatment varied significantly with period for total PMS scale ($F = 6.70, P < .01$), somatic symptoms scale ($F = 8.71, P < .001$), and psychological symptoms scale ($F = 3.50, P < .05$). With regard to the total PMS scale of the true reflexology and placebo reflexology groups, there was a significant repeated measures analysis of variance group-by-period interaction effect with paired comparisons of the baseline and reflexology treatment periods ($F = 13.2, P < .001$) and the baseline and post-treatment periods ($F = 7.7, P < .01$). Thus, the greater decrease in premenstrual symptoms by true reflexology was highly significant during the 8 weeks of reflexology sessions and for the next 2 months after treatment was terminated.

	True Reflexology	Placebo Reflexology
Mean Age (y)	37.2	32.7
Ethnic Status		
White	17 (94%)	12 (71%)
Hispanic	1 (6%)	2 (12%)
Black	0	2 (12%)
Other	0	1 (6%)
Marital Status		
Single	10 (56%)	10 (59%)
Married	3 (17%)	5 (29%)
Divorced	5 (28%)	2 (12%)
No. of Children		
None	11 (61%)	12 (71%)
One	2 (11%)	4 (23%)
Several	5 (28%)	1 (6%)
Education Level		
High School	1 (6%)	2 (12%)
Some College	10 (56%)	6 (35%)
Bachelor's Degree	2 (11%)	6 (35%)
Graduate Degree	5 (28%)	3 (18%)
Annual Income		
$1,000-15,000	1 (6%)	3 (18%)
$16,000-25,000	5 (28%)	4 (23%)
$26,000-40,000	7 (39%)	8 (47%)
$41,000-60,000	3 (17%)	2 (12%)
≥$61,000	2 (11%)	0

Table 1. Characteristics of Participants at Entry

Scale	Reflexology Group	Placebo Group	P
Total PMS			
Baseline	6.6 ± 2.7	6.3 ± 2.8	
Treatment	3.6 ± 1.9	5.0 ± 2.4	13.2*
Post-treatment	4.1 ± 2.6	5.2 ± 2.5	7.7*
Somatic Symptoms			
Baseline	7.0 ± 2.2	6.0 ± 2.6	
Treatment	4.0 ± 2.0	4.9 ± 2.1	19.6*
Post-treatment	4.6 ± 2.4	5.1 ± 2.3	8.3*
Psychological Symptoms			
Baseline	6.2 ± 3.7	6.6 ± 3.3	
Treatment	3.1 ± 2.1	5.2 ± 3.0	6.4†
Post-treatment	3.6 ± 3.0	5.4 ± 2.9	4.2†

PMS = Premenstrual Syndrome.　　　　　　　　　　　* p < .01.
Data are Presented as Mean ± SD.　　　　　　　　　† p < .05.

Table 2. Changes in Premenstrual Syndrome Across Treatment Periods by Reflexology Group

For the separate measures of somatic and psychological symptoms, the pattern was similar. The repeated-measures analysis for the somatic symptoms scale was statistically significant for group-by-period interactions comparing the baseline period to the treatment period ($F = 19.6$, $P < .001$) and for paired comparisons of the baseline period to the post-treatment period ($F = 8.3$, $P < .01$). Likewise, the repeated-measures analysis for the psychological symptoms scale showed a significant interaction effect between the treatment groups for the difference between the baseline and reflexology periods ($F = 6.4$, $P < .05$) and between the baseline and post-treatment periods ($F = 4.2$, $P < .05$).

The greatest mean percent change in the total PMS scale scores from the baseline conditions to the treatment period was the 46% reduction shown by the true reflexology group, which remained relatively the same (41%) during the post-treatment period. The 19% change from baseline conditions for the placebo reflexology group was less than half that shown by the true reflexology subjects. Similar patterns were also demonstrated by the percent changes in somatic and psychological symptoms. The respective decreases from the baseline to the treatment periods shown by the true reflexology and placebo reflexology groups were 43 and 17% for the somatic symptoms scale and 50 and 22% for the psychological symptoms scale, respectively. Examining individual participants, 15 (83%) of the 18 women in the true reflexology group showed at least a 30% decrease in total PMS scores during the 8-week reflexology treatment period, whereas only four (24%) of the 17 women in the placebo reflexology group exhibited such a reduction. This difference between the groups is significant by χ^2 test ($\chi^2 = 10.8$, $P < .01$).

Discussion

This randomized controlled study showed that true reflexology treatment led to a significantly greater reduction in premenstrual symptoms than did placebo reflexology. Though there was a larger percent reduction in premenstrual symptoms during the treatment period, the significant difference between the treatment groups also persisted for 2 months after treatment for both somatic and psychological symptoms. Previous studies of medical management of PMS by pituitary gonadotropin hormones[6,7] and oral contraceptives[8,9] showed that these drugs significantly reduced physical premenstrual symptoms as compared to placebo treatment, but they were not as effective with psychological symptoms and often produced pronounced side effects when used on a long-term basis. Although psychotropic drugs improved mood-related premenstrual symptoms significantly more than placebo substances,[10-14] they have not proved as reliable in reducing the somatic symptoms that accompany PMS, and they also produce unwanted side effects. No negative side effects were reported with reflexology therapy; instead, most subjects found the treatment pleasant and relaxing.

Although no previous study has examined the role of reflexology in the treatment of premenstrual distress, Helms[21] conducted a randomized, controlled clinical trial on the effectiveness of acupuncture in managing primary dysmenorrhea. Over twice as many women showed a pronounced reduction in dysmenorrhea-related pain in the real acupuncture group as compared to a placebo acupuncture group, a standard medical treatment group, or a visitation control group. The participants in the real acupuncture group also reported a significantly greater reduction in analgesic medication use than subjects in the other groups. As in previous research, Helms postulated that the benefits of acupuncture might be related to alterations in adrenal, gonadal, and pituitary activity, as well as to possible acupuncture-induced changes in sympathetic autonomic nervous system activity, endogenous opioid release, and prostaglandin levels. Because Dale[16] noted that the micro-acupuncture systems on the ear, hand, and foot correlate to the macro-acupuncture systems described by the Chinese, similar physiologic mechanisms may account for the clinical benefits of acupuncture and reflexology.

The theoretical rationale for the study of Goodale et al,[15] which examined the physiologic mechanisms for the effectiveness of relaxation therapy, may also apply to the present study. Goodale et al proposed that relaxation training reduces the psychophysiologic response to stress and that reduction of stress helps alleviate PMS. Even though baseline serum cortisol levels are relatively stable over the menstrual cycle, Marinari et al[22] found that women tested premenstrually exhibited greater adrenocortical reactivity to psychological distress than those tested at mid-cycle. As acupuncture has been shown to reduce plasma ACTH and cortisol levels,[23] reflexology could also serve to attenuate adrenocortical stress reactivity. It is not as obvious why the benefits of reflexology were maintained for 2 months post-treatment, but one possibility is that the brain mechanisms[24] related to acupuncture and to the reflexology micro-systems can be altered permanently by the treatment.

The primary benefit reported by the women receiving true reflexology therapy was the experience of profound relaxation. Many of the women fell asleep during the 30-minute reflexology session and reported having more energy the next day. This finding corresponds to the extensive survey by Pullon et al,[3] which noted that some type of massage therapy was the single most effective self-help treatment reported by women for relief of premenstrual symptoms. Massage, rest, and exercise received a higher rating of success for alleviating PMS than did the medications prescribed by physicians.

One of the greatest experimental difficulties in designing this research was the development of a credible placebo control group. Every effort was made to present the placebo reflexology session as a potentially beneficial treatment, without actually providing therapeutically effective reflexology therapy. It was particularly difficult for the volunteer reflexology therapists not to touch appropriate areas of the ears, hands, and feet therapeutically when the women in the placebo control group complained of severe premenstrual distress. Even though the type of manual pressure given to the placebo subjects was either overly light or very rough, the participants in the placebo reflexology group consistently commented during their sessions that they found the therapy relaxing and pleasant. Many of these women reported that they enjoyed lying down for half an hour and having someone else attend to them. Although some of these placebo subjects stated that they thought the reflexology was "having an effect," their daily diaries did not indicate as large a reduction in premenstrual symptoms from baseline values as did the participants in the true reflexology group.

Some investigators[4,14] have suggested that there is a high placebo response for PMS patients, but other studies[8,10,12,13] have reported that the reduction in premenstrual symptoms for placebo subjects was less than 20%. This figure is comparable to the 19% change in PMS severity found for our subjects who received placebo reflexology. At the same time, other studies have indicated higher levels of benefit from the experimental treatment than was found for reflexology. The 46% reduction in premenstrual symptoms in the true reflexology subjects is lower than the 58% improvement found by Goodale et al[15] for women trained to produce the relaxation response. Moreover, medication management of PMS has achieved successes in 60-75%.[6,13] Unfortunately, all of these studies used different assessment measures for evaluating PMS. A clinically controlled comparison of several different therapies for women given the same PMS assessment form would be valuable future research.

References

1. Frank RT. The hormonal causes of premenstrual tension. Arch Neurol Psychiatry 1931; 26: 1053-7.

2. Nader S. Premenstrual syndrome: Tailoring treatment to symptoms. Postgrad Med 1991; 90: 173-8.

3. Pullon SR, Reinken JA, Sparrow MJ. Treatment of premenstrual symptoms in Wellington women. N Z Med J 1989; 102: 72-4.

4. Freeman EW, Rickels K, Sondheimer SJ, Polansky M. Ineffectiveness of progesterone suppository treatment for premenstrual syndrome. JAMA 1990; 264: 349-53.

5. Freeman EW, Rickels K, Sondheimer SJ. Course of premenstrual syndrome severity after treatment. Am J Psychiatry 1992; 149: 531-3.

6. Mortola JF, Girton L, Fischer U. Successful treatment of severe premenstrual syndrome by combined use of gonadotropinreleasing hormone agonist and estrogen / progestin. J Clin Endocrinol Metab 1991; 72: 252A-F.

7. Muse KN, Cetel NS, Futterman LA, et al. The premenstrual syndrome. Effect of "medical ovariectomy." N Engl J Med 1984; 311: 1345-9.

8. Deeny M, Hawthorn R, Hart DM. Low dose danazol in the treatment of the premenstrual syndrome. Postgrad Med J 1991; 67: 450-4.

9. Graham CA, Sherwin BB. A prospective treatment study of premenstrual symptoms using a triphasic oral contraceptive. J Psychosom Res 1992; 36: 257-66.

10. Smith S, Rinehart JS, Ruddock VE, Schiff I. Treatment of premenstrual syndrome with alprazolam: Results of a double-blind, placebo-controlled, randomized crossover clinical trial. Obstet Gynecol 1987; 70: 37-43.

11. Harrison WM, Endicott J, Nee J. *Treatment of premenstrual dysphoria with alprazolam.* Arch Gen Psychiatry *1990; 47: 270-5.*

12. Glick R, Harrison W, Endicott J, McGrath P, Quitkin FM. *Treatment of premenstrual dysphoric symptoms in depressed women.* J Am Med Wom Assoc *1991; 46: 182-5.*

13. Rickels K, Freeman EW, Sondheimer S, Albert J. *Fluoxetine in the treatment of premenstrual syndrome.* Curr Ther Res *1990; 48: 161-6.*

14. Sundblad C, Modigh K, Andersch B, Eriksson E. *Clomipramine effectively reduces premenstrual irritability and dysphoria: A placebo controlled trial.* Acta Psychiatr Scand *1992; 85: 39-47.*

15. Goodale IL, Domar AD, Benson H. *Alleviation of premenstrual syndrome symptoms.* Obstet Gynecol *1990; 75: 649-55.*

16. Dale RA. *The principles and systems of microacupuncture.* Int J Chin Med *1984; 1: 15-42.*

17. Oleson TD, Kroening RJ. *A comparison of Chinese and Nogier auricular acupuncture points.* Am J Acupuncture *1983; 12: 325-44.*

18. Oleson TD, Kroening RJ, Bresler DE. *An experimental evaluation of auricular diagnosis: The somatotopic mapping of musculoskeletal pain at ear acupuncture points.* Pain *1980; 8: 217-29.*

19. Isaac S, Michaels WB. Handbook in Research and Evaluation. *San Diego: Edits Publishers, 1975.*

20. Cook TD, Campbell DT. Quasi-Experimentation: Design and Analysis Issues for Field Settings. *Boston: Houghton Mifflin, 1979.*

21. Helms JM. *Acupuncture for the management of primary dysmenorrhea.* Obstet Gynecol *1987; 69: 51-6.*

22. Marinari KT, Leshner AI, Doyle MP. *Menstrual cycle status and adrenocortical reactivity to stress.* Psychoneuroendocrinology *1976; 1: 213-8.*

23. Wen HL, Ho WK, Wong HK, Mehal ZD, Ng YH, Ma L. *Reduction of adrenocorticotropic hormone (ACTH) and cortisol in drug addicts treated by acupuncture and electrical stimulation (AES).* Comp Med East West *1978; 6: 61-6.*

24. Bossy J. *Neural mechanisms in acupuncture analgesia.* Minerva Med *1979; 70: 1705-15.*

Critical Evaluation

- ## Comments on the Abstract

What information, if any, is missing?

This article uses a standardized abstract. Most of the information is clearly laid out—the research question as well as a good description of the subjects and methods used. However, given the amount of self-reporting that subjects were required to do (the six months of daily diary-keeping), a careful reader will plan to check to see what steps the authors took to monitor subjects' recordkeeping, and how any missing data was handled. In addition, the actual numbers of the results are not stated.

- ## Comments on the Introduction

Is the study objective clearly stated?

Yes, very clearly.

Are the study's context and relevance clearly established?

Yes. The authors make a case for how widespread discomfort related to PMS is among women. They also describe in detail previous studies on PMS and exactly how this study will build upon what has been previously learned.

- ## Comments on the Methods Section

Is the sample well described, including inclusion/exclusion criteria and method of selection?

Yes, inclusion and exclusion criteria are clearly defined and make sense. The method of selection, newspaper advertisements, allows for a fairly wide cross-section of potential subjects. The ability to read a newspaper is not correlated in any meaningful way with PMS, so this method of selection should not bias the results.

Are blinding procedures used, and if so, how well did they work?

Yes, blinding was used, since subjects did not know which group they had been assigned to. The authors checked with the subjects and found that all of them thought they had received actual reflexology therapy, so the blinding method appears to have worked.

Is a comparison or placebo group part of the design?

Yes. This study is one of the few that has used a placebo touch treatment, consisting of uneven pressure applied to points considered not appropriate for the treatment of PMS. In the context of the research hypothesis, it seems well designed.

Is the treatment procedure well described and appropriate given the hypothesis?

Yes. If a reader were planning to replicate this intervention study or to design one similar to it, there is enough information here to do so. The description of the true and sham reflexology treatments is very thorough.

Is treatment randomly assigned, and is the method of randomization described?

Yes, treatment was randomly assigned using a table of random numbers.

Are the outcome measures well described and appropriate given the hypothesis?

Yes, they appear to be, based on the literature cited. The inclusion of both physiological and psychological symptoms is a plus. The authors have also gone to some trouble to verify that the symptom diary used as the primary measure is both a valid and reliable measure, as shown by the tests for internal consistency, test-retest reliability, and correlation with another similar measure, the Health Distress Index.

Are the methods used in calculating both descriptive and inferential statistical analysis described?

Only the methods used for calculating inferential statistics are described. It appears that the plans for analysis were specified in advance but this is not entirely clear from reading the methods section. As mentioned previously, stating the plan for statistical analysis in advance enhances the credibility of a study's results by avoiding 'fishing expeditions,' where multiple tests are performed on the data in an effort to find meaningful patterns.

• Comments on the Results Section

Are the tables and graphs clearly labeled?

Yes, these are straightforward and easy to read.

Are all the participants accounted for?

Yes. Notice the high rate of attrition, 33 out of the original 83 who entered the study plus an additional 15 after subjects had been assigned to group. This means that 48 of the 83 participants dropped out, a rate that is over 50%. While it is not surprising that a large number of subjects would drop out of a study with such lengthy evaluation and treatment periods, it is important to ask whether the subjects who remained might share a common characteristic that could bias the results in some way. In this instance it is difficult to tell—perhaps the subjects with the greater amount of patience needed to complete the study were more likely to report positive results because they had invested so much time and energy to participate, or perhaps those experiencing benefit were more likely to stay with the study. A shortcoming is that the authors do not identify the number of dropouts for each group.

Are means and standard deviations provided?

Yes, means and standard deviations are provided. Notice that the standard deviations are relatively smaller than the means, so there is low individual variation in the results, making it more likely that the reduction in symptoms of PMS is really a consequence of the treatment. Compare these means and standard deviations to those reported in the previous example.

What results of statistical analyses are provided?

Both the results of demographic data and inferential analysis of the scale scores for each group are included. Notice however, that wherever possible the authors report results in terms of percentages rather than the raw numbers. Which sounds more impressive, 50% or five out of ten? Always check the numbers upon which the reported percentages are based.

Are all the research outcomes previously specified reported?

Yes.

•   Comments on the Discussion Section

Are the authors' comments justified, based on the results?

Yes, most of the time. The discussion of possible mechanisms is both engaging and logical. The discussion of the placebo control is also interesting, but could have been explored further, particularly regarding the difficulties experienced by the therapists who provided the sham intervention. More qualitative information on this aspect of the study would have enriched this section. The speculation that brain mechanisms involved in acupuncture and thus by implication, reflexology, can be permanently altered by these treatments may be a bit of a stretch.

Do the conclusions follow logically from the results?

Yes, it appears that the reflexology treatment did reduce PMS symptoms, based on the caliber of the design and the strength of the statistical results.

Do the authors identify weaknesses or limitations in the study design or analysis?

Yes, in the discussion of the possibility of placebo response and the lack of a common outcome measure for assessing PMS. However, more discussion of the possibility of a 'nocebo' response in the sham treatment group, due to the therapists' discomfort with providing an ineffective treatment and whether this may have been unconsciously communicated to participants, would have enriched this section.

Is the clinical significance of the study discussed?

Briefly. The study results support the use of reflexology in treating PMS, particularly because it addresses both physiological and psychological symptoms, and does not have the side effects of medications.

Are the conclusions consistent with the study objectives?

Yes, overall. The study hypothesis and objectives are clearly stated, and the design and the methods used are congruent with these. Contrast the strength of the design and the appropriateness of the methods, especially the reflexology protocol, with those in the previous study on massage and cancer pain.

• Comments on the Reference List

How up to date and adequate is the reference list?

Both up to date and adequate—the citations seem both pertinent and succinct.

Did the authors examine other articles focusing on similar designs, populations, and outcomes?

It is difficult to tell. Most of the references seem to be related to documenting the problems associated with PMS, and to studies on medications used in treating it.

Based on the results of this study, would you make any changes in your practice?

A massage therapist with training in reflexology could certainly consider incorporating manipulation of the identified points for clients who report PMS symptoms. Although it is not perfect, this is a well-designed and thoughtfully conducted study. A careful reader can have a fairly high degree of confidence that the observed results are an effect of the treatment. The massage therapist without reflexology training may feel more comfortable making referrals to a reflexologist.

Summary

Evaluating health care research critically takes knowledge and practical skills. In the last two chapters we have developed a protocol for systematically reading and critiquing a quantitative study. Putting into practice what you have learned, you now have the ability to improve the quality of the care you provide to your clients through integrating new research information. Be reasonably skeptical, realizing that no study is perfect, and that researchers often face a number of practical challenges which can limit their results. But also recognize that these are factors that have the potential to reduce the validity and reliability of a study. In the next chapter, we will learn how to read and evaluate a qualitative study.

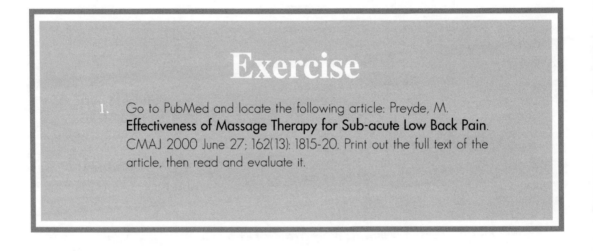

Exercise

1. Go to PubMed and locate the following article: Preyde, M. **Effectiveness of Massage Therapy for Sub-acute Low Back Pain**. CMAJ 2000 June 27; 162(13): 1815-20. Print out the full text of the article, then read and evaluate it.

Chapter 7

How to Read a Qualitative Article

A scientist is, then, a seeker after truth. The truth is that which he reaches out for, the direction toward which his face is turned. Complete certainty is beyond his reach, though, and many questions to which he would like answers lie outside the universe of discourse of natural science.

P. B. Medawar

Learning Objectives

- Describe the major differences between qualitative and quantitative research paradigms.

- Name three types of qualitative approaches and their theoretical basis.

- List three design strategies that enhance the trustworthiness of qualitative research.

- Practice critiquing a qualitative study.

Qualitative Inquiry

As we discussed in Chapter 1, qualitative methods were developed largely out of the need for a different approach to answering questions of interest in the social sciences. Many important and useful questions cannot be answered using quantitative methods. For example, "What proportion and demographic segments of the public use complementary therapies?" clearly requires a quantitative approach, but "How do people decide to seek a complementary practitioner?" is a different kind of question that necessitates a qualitative strategy.

Although qualitative research has historically been the domain of social scientists like anthropologists and sociologists, qualitative methods are now being used more often by biomedical researchers to give depth and understanding to their quantitative work. While developing a written survey to assess smoking behavior, for example, a researcher conducted focus groups with smokers and found that the researcher's use of the term "quit", which was intended to convey a decision to stop smoking permanently, was actually used by smokers to refer to a temporary break from smoking. Had the researcher not incorporated qualitative methodology into the design of her study, the survey instrument would have been fatally flawed, and she would have unknowingly reached an erroneous conclusion.

Qualitative methods are especially useful when exploring uncharted territory because variables of interest may be poorly understood, ill-defined, or uncontrollable. The qualitative approach has a great deal to offer in the exploration of complementary therapies, where so much is still unknown.

Qualitative methods are based on a divergent set of assumptions from quantitative methods. These assumptions include the idea that there is no single 'objective' reality and that there may be multiple equally valid realities, that the observer affects the phenomena observed, and that what is true in one situation or context may not necessarily be generalizable to other situations or contexts.

According to Michael Quinn Patton[1], qualitative inquiry is also distinguished by its use of several themes. These include:

- an emphasis on studying situations as they occur naturally, without manipulation by the researcher, and studying them as unobtrusively as possible;

- an openness to emergent design, where outcomes are not predetermined but are instead allowed to develop from immersion in the collected material—design strategies may change as the researcher's understanding of a process deepens, or in response as a situation changes;

- an emphasis on detailed description (referred to as "thick" or "rich" description) that includes direct quotations which portray participants' views and experiences;

- valuing the personal insights and experiences of the researcher, recognizing that while complete objectivity is impossible, a neutral attitude toward whatever content emerges is essential—the researcher has no personal axe to grind. While the qualitative researcher's experience is inevitably colored by culture, education, and personal beliefs, he or she recognises that the challenge is to suspend these as much as possible when observing and reporting. Analysis and interpretation of the data must be grounded in and supported by the data.

Types of Qualitative Approaches

There is no single qualitative method. Qualitative methods have been developed based on diverse approaches to knowledge used in fields such as anthropology, sociology, psychology, education, and philosophy. There are many different theoretical bases that provide a methodological foundation for qualitative approaches; we will mention some of the more commonly used ones here.

• *Grounded Theory*

Grounded theory is rooted in sociology. It was developed to help better understand human behavior through generating explanatory models[2] based on empirical data. Using grounded theory to investigate an identified phenomenon, say for example what massage therapy students undergo as they develop their professional identity, a researcher would select knowledgeable participants, and then systematically sample, collect and analyze data throughout the course of the study, primarily through interviews and participant observation. As a picture of the phenomenon begins to develop, the researcher continues to sample, collect, and analyze data, based on the emergent theory. Grounded theory is an ongoing and highly responsive process. Its strength is that the generated theories and models are strongly rooted in the data, and they continue to be revised as more data becomes available. This type of continuous revision is called an **iterative** process.

A feature of grounded theory that is sometimes incorporated into other approaches is the use of negative cases. Negative cases are contrary to the prevailing data and are purposefully sought out by the researcher to provide a different and more complete perspective. These can sometimes be the exception that proves the rule, and their presence increases the credibility of a study's findings.

• *Ethnography*

Ethnography developed from anthropology and relies on that field's traditional use of participant observation and fieldwork methods, that is, immersion in a **culture**. It is based on the assumption that any group of people will, over time, develop a culture. Ethnography answers the question: "What is the culture of this group?" Culture is a particular way of defining the world, the relationship of the group to it and to each other, and accepted standards of behavior, such as the proper way to make a request between members compared to non-members of the group. By this definition, the idea of culture is not limited to geographic location or ethnic heritage but can refer to any group of people, for example organizations, religious groups, or people in schools or workplaces. Ethnographic techniques could be used to study the culture of a particular complementary therapy training program, or the culture of a hospital ward.

• *Phenomenology*

Phenomenology is based in the field of philosophy, and is sometimes seen as synonymous with qualitative methods. Its focus is the essence and structure of the experience of a phenomenon for a group of people. For example, what is the nature of the experience of becoming an acupuncturist? From a phenomenological perspective, there is no objective reality—the subjective details of the experience and the interpretation of its meaning are necessary to understand its essence. Different people may undergo different versions of becoming an acupuncturist, yet there are likely to be common threads or themes that identify various stages or regular features of the experience.

Trustworthiness in Qualitative Research

Lincoln and Guba[3] have identified four aspects of trustworthiness in qualitative research, which they believe can be applied equally to all types of qualitative studies (and to quantitative studies as well). These are: truth value, or credibility; transferability; consistency; and neutrality, or confirmability. The rigor of qualitative research depends on attention to these factors.

• *Credibility*

Analogous to internal validity, credibility in qualitative research is based on describing and reporting the perspectives of study participants as clearly and as accurately as possible.

• *Transferability*

Similar to generalizability, this criterion refers to the capacity of the study findings to be applied to other contexts, settings, or groups. Although it can add to the utility of any study, transferability is not required for a qualitative study to be credible. Because qualitative research often emphasizes the unique nature of a situation, what is true in one setting or among one set of group members may not necessarily be true in other similar circumstances. In terms of applying results to clinical practice, a qualitative study may provide insight into the nature of client experience or give a practitioner a different or broader perspective on a particular issue. In this way, a study without high levels of transferability can still have clinical relevance.

• *Consistency*

This is the qualitative equivalent of reliability, that is, consistency over a period of time, or across groups or settings. The study data is internally congruent. As with transferability, the emphasis on unique experience in much qualitative research means that this type of consistency may not always be relevant, depending upon the nature of the particular study.

However, another type of consistency can be seen in qualitative studies where researchers employ **triangulation**. Triangulation refers to the use of multiple methods of data collection, or methods of analysis, or analysts. For example, a study might employ participant observation by the researcher together with interviews with knowledgeable informants conducted by other members of the research team. When there is consistency among the study results using multiple methods of data collection or analysis, confidence that the study findings are an accurate reflection of the phenomenon being studied is increased.

- *Neutrality*

This criterion relates to freedom from bias in the research process and in the reporting of results. Neutrality can be increased by studying participants over a longer period of time or through prolonged contact with them, including with negative cases, in order to gain a broader perspective and collect as much information or differing points of view as possible. The researcher can also attempt to identify his or her own biases by keeping a written journal where possible biases are noted, and through consultation with other researchers. The use of negative cases is a design feature that increases neutrality.

Evaluating Qualitative Research

Patton[1] succinctly identifies the following areas of evaluation for readers of qualitative research:

1. The use of rigorous and appropriate methods for collecting high-quality data, and for analyzing the data, that address issues related to validity and reliability.

2. The qualifications of the researcher—clearly training and experience are important, as well as track record, status in the field, and methods of self presentation in the research situation. The researcher is the instrument of data collection and is the core of the process of data analysis.

3. An appreciation, familiarity, and degree of comfort with the assumptions of the qualitative paradigm, including naturalistic inquiry, holistic thinking, and the use of qualitative approaches.

Based on these criteria, there are several basic questions to consider when reading any qualitative study and evaluating its trustworthiness. Most will sound familiar because they are inherently the same as those used in evaluating quantitative research.

While the methods used in qualitative research are quite different from those used in quantitative studies, they can be applied as rigorously. It is just as important in a qualitative study that the

Critical Evaluation Questions

1. Is the research question clearly articulated?

2. What assumptions underlie the study; what model or paradigm forms its theoretical basis?

3. What are the qualifications, experience, and perspective of the researcher(s)?

4. What techniques and methods were used to ensure the integrity of the results as well as their validity and accuracy? Are the methods used in data collection and analysis described in sufficient detail?

5. Given the theoretical model and the purpose of the study, are the methods used appropriate?

6. Are the results credible?

7. Do the results justify the conclusions?

8. Can the results be generalized to other settings? Are they clinically meaningful?

research question be clearly formulated as it is in a quantitative study. The care with which data is collected and analyzed is equally if not more crucial in a qualitative study. In collecting interview data, it is common to tape interviews for later transcription while the researcher also makes written notes about nonverbal behavior or nuances that cannot be captured on an audiotape. Coding for themes or patterns in interview data is often assisted by the use of computer programs that sort responses based on criteria such as key words or phrases. Methods used for data collection and analysis, including the use of any software package, should be spelled out in sufficient detail for the reader to understand what was done, and why[4].

Other considerations in evaluating quantitative research, such as the clarity and thoroughness of a review of the literature or the appropriateness of the references cited may also be relevant, depending on the individual study.

As you read the following study, think specifically about the questions listed in the box above.

Study Example:

Mastectomy, Body Image and Therapeutic Massage: A Qualitative Study of Women's Experience

Bredin, Mary MA RGN

Macmillan Research Practitioner, Macmillan Practice Development Unit, Centre for Cancer and Palliative Care Studies, Institute of Cancer Research at the Royal Marsden Hospital NHS Trust, London, UK

Accepted for publication 24 June 1998.

Correspondence: Mary Bredin MA, RGN, Macmillan Research Practitioner, Macmillan Practice Development Unit, Centre for Cancer and Palliative Care Studies, Institute of Cancer Research at the Royal Marsden Hospital, Fulham Road, London SW3 6JJ, UK. E-mail: maryb@ICR.ac.uk

Full Text of: Bredin: J Adv Nurs, Volume 29(5). May 1999. 1113-1120 Journal of Advanced Nursing © 1999 Blackwell Science Ltd.

Abstract

Despite the wealth of literature concerning the impact of breast loss on a woman's body image, sexual and psychological adjustment, there have been few studies within the medical and nursing literature directly quoting a woman's private perspective; how in her words she experiences her changed body. Furthermore, there is a lack of evidence-based interventions for addressing the problem of altered body image (ABI); healthcare professionals often feel at a loss in knowing how to help women cope (Hopwood & Maguire 1998)[11]. In this study in-depth interviews were undertaken to explore three women's experiences of breast loss with particular focus on body image issues; a second phase piloted a massage intervention as a means of helping them adjust to living with their changed body image. Listening to their experience, in combination with the therapeutic massage, allowed deep access and insight into the nature of the women's trauma. The experiences of the three women in this study suggest there may be a group of women whose needs are overlooked and who, despite their prosthesis and reassurances that they are disease-free, opt to conceal the problems they have in living with a changed image. The availability of a body-centred therapy might help with certain aspects of adjustment as revealed by this study.

Introduction

A great deal has been written and researched on the psychological and social effects of mastectomy. This research has shown that whereas all cancer causes anxiety about the disease and its progression, mastectomy threatens some women with a distressing disturbance of body image, partly because of the breast's symbolic and physical association with being a woman.

This paper reports on a qualitative study which explored three women's experiences of breast cancer with a particular focus on body image issues. The study incorporated two phases; the first phase was to interview three women about their experiences of mastectomy, and a second phase offered each woman a body-centred intervention involving massage and listening, as a means of helping them adjust to their changed body image. While the study shows that the women's distress was clearly multi-dimensional, it also revealed that their bodily loss remained a potent focus for their distress and a reminder of a wider sense of disruption. According to the women's accounts the intervention in some ways met their need to reveal (implicitly and explicitly) their secret loss and sense of being different.

Background: The Issue of Body Image Within Breast Cancer Research

In the light of the breast's emotional and symbolic significance much has been written about the impact of its loss through breast cancer. The literature on breast cancer which includes assessment of altered body image (ABI) is generally concerned with the psychological and psycho-social effects of mastectomy compared with breast conservation, adjuvant treatment and breast reconstruction (Fallowfield et al. 1986, Kemeny et al. 1988)[5,14]. These studies found that women have a more satisfactory body image following breast conservation; a fairly consistent finding despite the researchers offering no clear definition of body image nor standardized inventories to measure it (Schover et al. 1995). While it appears that women receiving conservative breast surgery report improved body image ratings, studies assessing the effects of surgery on psychological morbidity show similar levels of anxiety and depression regardless of the treatment given (Fallowfield & Hall 1991)[6]. Furthermore, the advantage women may gain in terms of greater body image satisfaction following breast conservation may be offset by an increased fear of cancer and its possible recurrence (Fallowfield et al. 1986)[5].

The supposition that fear about breast loss may take precedence over the fear of having a diagnosis of cancer may be erroneous, according to Fallowfield & Hall (1991)[6]. They explored this issue with a sample of 269 women in a prospective multi-centre study designed to evaluate the psychological outcome of different treatment policies in women with early breast cancer (Fallowfield et al. 1990)[7]. At the first post-operative interview the majority (159/244) gave 'fear of cancer' as their primary fear rather than the fear of losing a breast; only 12% of the sample (18 women who received mastectomy and 14 who received lumpectomy) felt that losing a breast was worse. This finding is similar to that of an earlier study by Peters-Golden (1982)[19] who examined perceptions of social support among 100 breast cancer patients and 100 disease-free individuals. Within the breast cancer group recurrence and spread of cancer and the consequences of treatment regimes took precedence over fears of losing a breast. Peters-Golden commented that researchers' assumptions that breast loss is the primary concern for women facing breast cancer may only serve to detract from the gravity of facing a life-threatening illness. Undoubtedly, these issues are blurred and for each woman reactions will vary considerably, depending on the emotional significance a woman attributes to her breast and her ability to adjust to having a life-threatening disease. Priorities at diagnosis and following treatment can change in significance over time; healthcare professionals need to be aware of this so that they can respond appropriately regardless of the nature of problems encountered.

Some of the earliest studies of mastectomy and body image explored whether mastectomy resulted in a negative body image (Polivy 1977, Jamison et al. 1978)[20,12]. For example, Polivy (1977)[20] examined the impact of mastectomy on feminine self-concept and body image. An important finding from this study was that immediately following surgery, mastectomy patients showed no body image alteration whereas patients undergoing breast biopsy showed a decline in body image and self-image. She suggested that both these groups used denial as a defence mechanism. However, for those women who learned their results were negative denial was no longer needed, therefore their self-image scores worsened post-operatively, while scores of those who had mastectomy showed little change. In contrast, 6-11 months after mastectomy significantly worse scores for body image and total self-image were evident. Polivy concluded that breast cancer and its treatment by total breast amputation are intrinsically both more anxiety-provoking and likely to leave a woman feeling worse about her body. However, she also commented that denial was an important part of the defence process whereby a woman who has undergone a mastectomy integrates her changed body into her new self-image.

In contrast to Polivy's (1977)[20] findings, it has been argued that many women will not always suffer irreparably as a consequence of mastectomy (Price 1990)[21]. Price (1990)[21] cites Anderson (1988)[1] who reported that women who had undergone mastectomy apparently recovered remarkably well, despite a lack of structured support. Some felt positively about the experience because it had removed the threat of the cancer. Confirming Anderson's (1988)[1] finding, Krouse & Krouse (1982)[15] examined a small sample of women: breast cancer patients (n = 9); gynaecological cancer patients (n = 5); and a non-cancer comparison group (n = 5). Assessments of depression and body image in the mastectomy group at 1, 2 and 20 months showed that after a brief initial crisis there was a total adaptation by the end of the study. In contrast, patients with gynaecological cancer had increased feelings of depression and worsening body image scores even at 20 months following surgery. However, it is not clear from the study what the authors mean by 'adaptation' and the small sample size makes it difficult to generalize the findings. More recently, Schover et al. (1995) conducted a retrospective study comparing psycho-social adjustment, body image and sexual function in women who had either breast conservation (n = 72) or reconstruction (n = 146) for early stage disease. Overall, fewer than 20% of women reported poor adjustment on the domains measured which included psycho-social distress, body image and sexual satisfaction. The two groups did not differ greatly in their results; however, women who had undergone chemotherapy had more sexual dysfunction, poorer body image and psychological distress. The authors conclude that it is important to identify women at high risk for psycho-social distress and they suggest that screening should be routine for women undergoing chemotherapy or reporting having a troubled marital relationship, feeling unattractive, dissatisfaction with sexual relationships or poor social support.

To summarize, it seems that not all women will find living with a mastectomy problematic. None the less, when a body image problem does exist it may not be apparent to health professionals initially; patients are often afraid of admitting they have a problem. For their part, doctors and nurses may be reluctant to enquire, perhaps because they feel they lack the time or skills needed to cope with the distress that inquiry might reveal (Hopwood & Maguire 1988)[11]. The present study suggests that there may be a group of women who, following breast cancer treatment, fail to reveal ABI distress, possibly because it may become apparent months later, when 'life' is meant to be returning to some sense of normality.

Body Image: Theoretical Considerations

The concept 'body image' is a construct deriving from different dimensions of body experience. Many authors have attempted to define the 'body image' phenomenon, the earliest and most frequently quoted definition was formulated by the German neurologist Paul Schilder who wrote:

> "The image of the human body means the picture of our own body which we form in our mind, that is to say the way in which our body appears to ourselves" (Schilder 1950, p. 11)[25].

Schilder's definition implies the highly subjective nature of the body image: as an inner representation of how one thinks and feels about one's body it may bear no relationship to how one's body appears to others. This subjectivity is also shaped by cultural and social influences and incorporates both unconscious and conscious subjective experience (Cash & Pruzinsky 1990)[2]. These are important considerations when attempting to capture and assess a woman's experience of her changed body image. Such perceptions and feelings may not always be easily translated into language. They can be difficult to articulate when they remain embedded in the realm of 'body experience' and a 'body language' beyond conscious thoughts, words and concepts.

The Study and its Methods

The first phase of the study explored three women's experience of breast loss following mastectomy. In the second phase of the inquiry a body-orientated intervention (therapeutic massage) was offered to each woman. The sample size was limited to three participants because of the time required to undertake the massage intervention. Each woman who entered the study had been identified as having a body image problem by their consultant oncologist or breast care nurses. Because of the difficulties in defining what constitutes a 'body image problem,' it was agreed that there would be no specific selection criteria; practitioners invited women to take part who:

1. showed signs of having significant problems in adapting to the loss of their breast, and

2. revealed that they were particularly distressed about their changed appearance.

Making Sense of Research

Ethical permission was granted, and three women were invited to join the study. The women had to be currently cancer-free following mastectomy, aged between 25 and 65 years, and referred not later than 1 year after their original diagnosis.

Each woman participated in two 1-hour semistructured interviews and six sessions of therapeutic massage. The initial interview and subsequent massage sessions were conducted by the author. The follow-up interview was conducted by an independent researcher who focused on the effects of the massage intervention. Field notes were kept throughout and all interviews were taped and transcribed. Data analysis was undertaken following Guba & Lincoln's research methods (Guba & Lincoln 1985)[10].

The Massage Intervention

Each session began with talking for a short time, to gauge how the participant was feeling and to discuss concerns about the massage. Participants were offered a choice of where to be massaged: foot, arm, face or back, depending on preference. Sessions started with a short relaxation where the participant was invited to become aware of her breathing, notice how her body was feeling and to consciously let her limbs relax. The massage consisted of light gentle efflourage strokes only, and once completed the participant was encouraged to lie quietly. She would then be invited to talk for a short while if she so chose.

A Rationale for the Intervention

A rationale for the intervention was developed out of the author's prior experience of working with breast cancer patients. There were two components to the intervention;

1. Body Concept

An important aspect of adjusting to a changed body image may be the manner in which an individual describes or creates an account of her body in relation to self. This has been described by Price (1994)[22] as the 'conceptual element' of the body image construct which may feature in patients' accounts of their symptoms and coping style. When addressing ABI distress it may be important to help a woman articulate or express her body's story; the image of and feelings she has about her body and the meaning her breasts have held for her. If, as part of her story for instance, a woman conceptualizes her breast as being 'mutilated' or 'grotesque' it is likely that she will experience increased distress about her changed image. Because of her embarrassment and fear of being stigmatized, she may not want to draw attention to such feelings even though they may colour her whole experience. In such circumstances, it may be helpful for a person telling her story simply to have her experience heard and acknowledged by an empathic listener (Mitchell 1995)[16].

2. Body Perception

A second aspect of the body image relates to how we sense our bodies physically through sensations and feelings. If a mastectomy results in distorting surgical scars, pain, skin numbness and muscular tension for instance, this will colour a woman's experience of her body. There are a number of ways in which massage might affect body perception. For example, offering a woman structured touch within a safe therapeutic context might enable her to address the bodily dimension of her distress. By having another person 'touch the untouchable', i.e. her damaged body, a woman might begin to re-experience her traumatized body in a more positive way (Peters et al. 1996)[18]. Emotional suffering may itself be felt as physical pain and muscular tension (Pruzinsky 1990)[23]; massage can influence this (Ferrell-Torry & Glick 1992)[8]. Illness and disfigurement can lead to feelings of being different and unacceptable (Murphy 1987)[17]; touch is a type of communication that transcends the usual boundaries between people. It can enable a person to feel 'held', to feel safe and accepted (Corner et al. 1995)[3]. It can be a very immediate expression of another person's ability to tolerate the unacceptable.

Findings

Four key categories emerged from the data, as follows:

1. *The women's experience of their changed bodies.*
2. *The effects of breast loss on self.*
3. *Effects of breast loss on social identity.*
4. *Experiences of the massage.*

The findings from the first three categories reflected the multi-dimensional nature of the women's experience; they expressed loss and difference at every level of their being. These categories are not distinct; they tend to overlap with each other, indicating the complexity of the subject matter. The fourth category, 'experiences of the massage,' directly reflected questions asked in the second interview about the women's experience of the intervention.

Women's Experiences of Their Changed Bodies

Each woman spoke of how she perceived and experienced her body—changes not only in sensations to the breast area but also within her whole body. For example, they all mentioned a variety of physical perceptions: numbness, coldness, skin sensitivity, stiffness, soreness, pain and lymphoedema in the arms. These were all unpleasant sensations which served as a constant reminder of their mastectomy experience. For example, 'Jane' was troubled by the sensitivity of her skin around her scar site. She was also affected by the change in the shape of her chest. The sense of the whole of her body feeling different made her self-conscious about her shape:

> *"You feel lopsided, there is no doubt about that and it's very strange when you haven't got the prosthesis on after a bath or moving in bed ... it's flat, it's noticeable ..."*

'Sarah' initially could not look at herself, preferring to take her baths in the dark:

> "Well, for three months I didn't even look at myself, I just put a lot of bubbles in the bath, I didn't look at all."

Four months after her mastectomy Sarah had managed to look at her breast but still did not like what she saw:

> "I don't like looking at it, if the towel falls down I just wrap it round it because I don't like looking at it."

'Vicky' had undergone a double mastectomy. Physically she experienced pain locally around her scar sites and was troubled by lymphoedema in both arms:

> "They [the arms] ache all the time and I'm in pain all the way down there all the time, and that rubs against your body so when I go down the road I have to hold my arms out."

Her body image had altered, but when Vicky was dressed she was less disturbed by this:

> "I think my scars are ugly. They are more grotesque than I thought they would be, I thought they would be a lot neater than they are ... and therefore my whole body shape is out of proportion. When you look in the mirror you look grotesque, but when I put my clothes on I don't give it a lot of thought."

For Sarah and Jane, difficulty in adapting may have been hindered by interpretations of their experience being like an 'amputation' or 'mutilation':

> "I suppose to an extent I feel deformed. That's probably the best way to describe it ... and your appearance has changed quite radically ... I think it's possibly one of the most mutilating things that a male or female can have done." [Jane]

Effects of Breast Loss on Self

It has been suggested that, as a consequence of western medicine's tendency to objectify the body and 'fix' the part that has gone wrong, a woman's breast has often been considered as detachable and replaceable (Young 1992)[28]. However, whether or not she likes her breasts, they are a part of her self-identity; the loss of one (or both) may feel as if she has lost a part of her self. The statements made in this category indicate that the women had experienced more than just a bodily change; something felt different at a deeper level of the self:

> "I know I don't look any different from the outside world but it's difficult to put into words; it's just there. You are different and there's no getting away from it." [Jane]

For Sarah, her breasts were deeply bound up with her womanly image. Speaking of her reflection in the mirror she commented:

> "I don't like it. That's not me any more."

Vicky acknowledged her sense of incompleteness and difference:

> "I am different. I had the most rounded boobs and I was proud of them. Although they were big, they were an important part of my life and now they are gone and yes there is this loss there—I feel diminished in some way but I couldn't tell you in what way; incomplete I suppose you would say."

Effects of Breast Loss on Social Identity

As an inner representation, the body image may bear no relationship to how a person's body appears to others. A person might feel, for example, that her body is ugly, beautiful, large or small at different times when in fact her external physical appearance has not changed. This subjectivity can be influenced by social interactions which in turn determine the body image and influence self-worth (Schain 1986, Foltz 1987)[24,9]. The women's statements suggested that their experience of breast loss had affected their social identity. All mentioned concealment, withdrawal, concern about others noticing, self-consciousness and changed behaviour with family/partners. Their statements indicated that they could cope as long as they kept up an appearance of looking normal by wearing their prosthesis and concealing their 'difference':

> ".... when I'm dressed I can cope with it. When I'm dressed nobody needs to know." [Sarah]

Jane felt different not only to herself but also in relation to other women:

> "I found it quite easy with my female friends on a one to one basis. But on a more than one to one basis I felt they are a woman and I am not, sort of thing. I don't know why, it's just the way you react I suppose."

Sarah felt uncomfortable with her partner:

> "I get sort of panicky if he goes to walk in the bathroom. I don't want him to touch me at the top at all ... because you are worried that he might touch the one that is not there ..."

Vicky did not have a partner but the idea of having another relationship was out of the question for her:

> "I think if there had been a thought at the back of mind of finding a mate prior to the operation there would be no thought now."

For each of the women there was an indication that they needed to hide the distress they felt from those around them; for example:

> "When my mum was here ... I couldn't wait for her to go so I could cry because I wasn't going to cry while she was here. When she went I just sat on the stairs and sobbed and sobbed." [Sarah]

Jane experienced conflict in not wanting to express how she felt:

> "I mean you sort of feel grateful in one way and guilty for feeling upset and different."

Experiences of the Massage

The findings within the fourth category showed that each woman had felt positive about the intervention. Despite precautions to avoid bias by using an outside researcher to conduct the second interviews, it is possible that the women may have felt less comfortable reporting negative experiences because of their relationship with the researcher/practitioner. However, there was no indication within the interview material or in their unrecorded communications that they had found the intervention unhelpful. In contrast, there were clear examples of how each woman had benefited from the sessions. Initially there was some apprehension about the intervention:

> "The first time I was very apprehensive because I wasn't sure ... and I always found it hard to relax ..."[Sarah]

Both Sarah and Vicky had suffered with numbness and pain in their arms as a consequence of their mastectomies. Sarah reported that the massage had helped her arm 'to feel part of her body' once more and Vicky had found it helpful in reducing discomfort in her arms:

> "You know there were days when I didn't know where to put my arms and yes the massage certainly helped my arms then ..."

All three women reported that the massage had helped them relax. For example, Sarah was surprised that she could let herself relax as she 'had always been one of those people who couldn't', Vicky reported that she would always 'had a lovely nap after the massage' and then she felt 'great'; Jane, too, was surprised at how it made her feel:

> "I just like the feeling of the massage and it did make me feel more relaxed. You know it sort of sends you off into another world almost its superb, I never would have imagined it would have that sort of effect..." [Jane]

Sarah and Vicky reported that they were sleeping better:

> "I wasn't sleeping at all, I mean every hour looking at the clock, but since my massage the last few weeks I've had good nights' sleep which I hadn't had for 8 months..." [Sarah]

Vicky was feeling more comfortable with touching her breast scars, and Sarah was able to look at herself once more:

> "When M. came I found touching my scars terrible, you know I didn't even touch them ... but now it does not bother me, I cream them and massage them and no problem." [Vicky]

"A few months back I'd covered myself up because I didn't like looking but I don't avoid the mirror as much as I would have before." [Sarah]

At times even gentle body-work such as therapeutic massage can 'open up' and bring to the surface previously suppressed emotions. This may be helpful, but practitioners also need to be aware that such a reaction may be potentially harmful. During the 6 weeks that Jane came for massage she had a period of feeling low - and it could be argued that the massage opened up feelings which previously she had suppressed:

"I had these couple of weeks of feeling pretty grim ... it was unfortunate that it happened while I was coming to see her but I think it was purely coincidental. On the other hand it might not have been ... I think it had to come out and I think it was important to do it really. I've certainly felt better since..."

Jane was given the choice to stop the sessions if she felt they were too disturbing because of feelings aroused. She chose to continue and talked about her grief of having cancer; in this way she was held physically and emotionally while she confronted feelings that had previously been too private and painful to reveal.

Sarah's dissatisfaction with her body and her fear of her partner's reaction to the sight of her breast had led her to conceal her wound totally. During the 6 weeks she came for the massage she resumed sexual relations with her partner, and she managed to show her breast to a friend:

"I didn't look at it for the couple of months myself anyway, now I look at it ... I mean I can cope now, I mean at one time a while back if a towel dropped off me I'd have been ... but now if it drops I don't ... And actually my friend I actually showed her the other week.

Vicky's story suggests that the intervention was an opportunity to be touched at a time when her body felt 'repulsive':

"Being that I haven't got a partner I am not touched ... I think I felt my body was a bit repulsive and therefore people would not want to touch me and I think the massage helped me ..."

She also had found it helpful to talk:

"I can't talk to the family and I haven't got a close personal relationship with somebody I could actually share so yes I shared it with M. and therefore she has helped me through quite a lot of feelings."

As well as talking about their massage experience, a strong theme to emerge from the second round of interviews was the women's ability to accept and cope with their changed self-images:

"You just learn to live with it in the same way you learn to live with other things, you know people with amputations and things like that I suppose. The same with

bereavement you don't get over it but you learn to cope with it and I think this is much the same." [Jane]

"Yes I've got used to my scars, I didn't like them at first I thought they were ugly. Well they are still not pretty but I've got used to them and I've accepted that they are there and it's the body I've got to live with now." [Vicky]

"Oh yes I'm feeling better because I suppose I'm coping with it better, accepting it I suppose that's all you can do." [Sarah]

Discussion

It is widely acknowledged that a small percentage of women will develop significant problems adjusting to their body image as a result of mastectomy. Body image distress can be experienced not just in terms of an impaired sense of femininity or sexuality; it can have a profound impact on the 'whole' of one's being (Coyler 1996)[4]. Revelation of distress may be hindered by a fear of stigma, as a consequence of living in a culture where womanhood is bound up with having a perfect body and blemish-free appearance. It is not easy for health-care professionals to become aware of the problem of ABI distress post-treatment since, as this study revealed, some women will try to conceal their loss, physically and emotionally, under an outward desire to be seen as 'normal'.

The current management of breast cancer aims to rid the body of the disease, and as yet there is no consistent approach to identifying women at risk of ABI. The issue may be compounded by the difficulty in defining what the term a 'body image problem' means. An implication from this study is the need for a working definition. Practitioners must to be able to differentiate 'normal' and 'abnormal' reactions to breast loss—practical assessment tools are also needed.

When distress is encountered, how can body image problems be treated? While there is evidence to suggest that specialist nurses can and do provide invaluable counselling and support for women identified with ABI (Watson et al. 1988, Wilkinson et al. 1988)[26,27] such resources are often stretched and practitioners may feel they are limited in what they can offer.

It appears, moreover, from the private experiences of the three women in this study that subjective body experience and 'shocking' emotions can be too shameful to voice and (in some cases) literally beyond words. Can healthcare professionals help women find a language to express bodily distress and discomfort? Perhaps the multi-dimensional nature of the experience needs to be taken into account so that nursing care can attend to the three dimensions of experience: body, self and interpersonal self. While it may simply be enough for a woman to disclose her story and have her feelings acknowledged, the availability of a body-centred approach such as therapeutic massage could be valuable for woman with ABI problems post-mastectomy. The findings from this study suggest this would be worth exploring in more depth.

The three cases presented in this study are not necessarily typical of how women respond to or cope with the loss of a breast. The findings cannot be generalized. The women took part in the study because they were having difficulty in coming to terms with their changed body images. Statements made in the second interview about 'coping better' cannot be attributed entirely to the intervention, since it is possible they might have adjusted in their own time without such support.

However, it appears from their statements that the intervention helped them in important ways to cope at a time when the body had become an 'unacceptable' object. It may, for example, have provided some containment for what was previously uncontainable (Judd 1993)[13]; the untouchable and unspeakable perceptions of a changed body. It provided an opportunity for the women (literally and figuratively) to reveal themselves, and talk at a time when they felt isolated in their distress. Finally, it may have helped reduce bodily tension and discomfort, enabling relaxation and promoting sleep.

This tentative exploration of a body-orientated intervention suggests there may be potential scope for introducing it into clinical practice, but it must be acknowledged that there would be several difficulties in doing so. The notion of introducing a complementary therapy such as massage into an area where there is a gap in conventional health care has implications. Like any intervention massage may be harmful. Few research studies exist demonstrating its efficacy and many professionals understandably consider it unsafe to refer a patient to an unknown and unproven resource. There are no clear guidelines for appropriate referral or contra-indications. For instance, the women in this study clearly had differing needs. According to their comments Sarah and Vicky found the massage helpful; Jane found the relaxation aspect useful too, but the massage itself may have been too physically and psychologically invasive, given her previous ways of coping. Undoubtedly, this type of intervention invites disclosure at a time when a woman's coping mechanisms might actually require her to deny her loss. Nursing research into this area is required and must be evaluated as part of an integrated approach to managing body image problems in breast cancer patients, about whose incidence we still know so little.

Conclusion

The experiences of the three women in this study are unique. Although not generalizable, the findings raise some important concerns and questions which challenge the approach currently adopted by healthcare practitioners. They imply that the current approach to managing women post-mastectomy may at times compound the experience of difference that leads some women to conceal their sense of loss inappropriately, with disturbing physical and emotional consequences. The immediate response to helping women adjust to their breast loss is to replace the irreplaceable: the prosthesis is fitted along with the reassurances that they are disease-free. Conventional management colludes with women's sense that their feelings of loss and disfigurement should be kept secret—the implicit imperative is to conform to being normal. It may be that this collusion between patients and professionals makes them pretend that adjustment is happening when in fact it is not.

As Jane's conflicting feelings implied, it was because she felt grateful to be rid of her cancer that she felt she should not express her anger and distress.

We should consider whether a body-centred intervention involving massage could be valuable in a multidisciplinary approach to preventing and treating distress after mastectomy. The findings from this study indicate that it introduced a clinically useful extra dimension which allowed significant disturbing experiences and feelings to be talked about, touched on, and met in a way that went beyond words.

Acknowledgements

With thanks to Dr. Tim Sheard and Dr. David Peters for their support and advice.

References

1. *Anderson J. (1988) Coming to terms with mastectomy.* Nursing Times *84, 41-44. Reprinted in* Body Image Nursing Concepts and Care *(Price B. ed.), Prentice Hall International Ltd, Herts (1990), pp. 235-239.*

2. *Cash T. & Pruzinsky T. (1990) Integrative themes in body-image development deviance and change. In:* Body Images Development, Deviance, and Change *(Cash T. & Pruzinsky T., eds), Guilford Press, London, Chapter 16, pp. 337-338.*

3. *Corner J., Cawley N. & Hildebrand S. (1995) An evaluation of the use of massage and massage with the addition of essential oils on the well-being of cancer patients. The Centre for Cancer and Palliative Care Studies, The Institute of Cancer Research, The Royal Marsden NHS Trust, London.*

4. *Coyler H. (1996) Women's experience of living with breast cancer.* Journal of Advanced Nursing *23, 496-501.*

5. *Fallowfield L.J., Baum M. & Maguire P. (1986) Effects of breast conservation on psychological morbidity associated with diagnosis of early breast cancer.* British Medical Journal *293, 1331-1334.*

6. *Fallowfield L.J. & Hall A. (1991) Psychosocial and sexual impact of diagnosis and treatment of breast cancer.* British Medical Bulletin *47, 388-399.*

7. *Fallowfield L.J., Hall A., Maguire G.P. & Baum M. (1990) Psychological outcomes of different treatment policies in women with early breast cancer outside a clinical trial.* British Medical Journal *301, 575-580.*

8. *Ferrell-Torry A. & Glick O. (1992) The use of therapeutic massage as a nursing intervention to modify anxiety and the perception of pain.* Cancer Nursing *16, 93-101.*

9. *Foltz A. (1987) The influence of cancer on self concept and life quality.* Seminars in Oncology Nursing *3, 303-312.*

10. *Guba E.G. & Lincoln Y.S. (1985)* Naturalistic Inquiry. *Sage, London.*

11. *Hopwood P. & Maguire G.P. (1988) Body image problems in cancer patients.* British Journal of Psychiatry *153, 47-50.*

12. *Jamison K.R., Wellisch D.K. & Pasnau R.O. (1978) Psychosocial aspects of mastectomy: I. The women's perspective.* American Journal of Psychiatry *135, 432-436.*

13. *Judd D. (1993) Life-threatening illness a psychic trauma: psychotherapy with adolescent patients. In:* The Imaginative Body—Psychodynamic Therapy in Health Care *(Erskine A. & Judd D., eds), Whurr Publishers, London, pp. 87-112.*

14. *Kemeny M.M., Wellisch D. & Schain W. (1988) Psychosocial outcome in randomised surgical trial for treatment of primary breast cancer.* Cancer *62, 1231-1237.*

15. *Krouse H. & Krouse J. (1982) Cancer as crisis: the critical elements of adjustment.* Nursing Research *31, 96-101.*

16. *Mitchell A. (1995) Therapeutic relationship in health care: towards a model of the process of treatment.* Journal of Interprofessional Care *9, 15-20.*

17. *Murphy R.F. (1987) The damaged self. In:* The Body Silent *(Murphy R.F. ed.), Dent and Sons Ltd, London, pp. 73-95.*

18. *Peters D., Bredin M., Daniel R. & Clover A. (1996) Clinical forum: breast cancer.* Complementary Therapies in Medicine *4, 178-184.*

19. *Peters-Golden H. (1982) Breast cancer: varied perceptions of social support in the illness experience.* Social Science in Medicine *16, 483-491.*

20. *Polivy J. (1977) Psychological effects of mastectomy on a woman's feminine self concept.* Journal of Nervous and Mental Disease *164, 77-87.*

21. *Price B. (1990)* Body Image Nursing Concepts and Care. *Prentice Hall International Ltd, Herts, pp. 235-239.*

22. *Price B. (1994) The asthma experience: altered body image and non-compliance.* Journal of Clinical Nursing *3, 139-145.*

23. *Pruzinsky T. (1990) Somatopsychic approaches to psychotherapy and personal growth. In:* Body Images Development, Deviance, and Change *(Cash T. & Pruzinsky T., eds), Guilford Press, London, pp. 296-315.*

24. *Schain W. (1986) Sexual functioning, self-esteem and cancer care. In:* Body-Image, Self-Esteem, and Sexuality in Cancer Patients *(Vaeth J.M., ed.), 2nd edn. Karger, Basel, pp. 15-23.*

25. *Schilder P. (1950)* The Image and Appearance of the Human Body. *International Universities Press, New York, p. 11.*

26. *Watson M., Denton S., Baum M. & Greer S. (1988) Counselling breast cancer patients: a specialist nurse service.* Counselling Psychology Quarterly *1, 25-33.*

27. *Wilkinson S., Maguire P. & Tait A. (1988) Life after breast cancer.* Nursing Times *84, 34-37.*

28. *Young M.I. (1992) The breasted experience: the look and the feeling. In:* The Body in Medical Thought and Practice *(Leder, D. ed.), Kluwer Academic Publishers, The Netherlands, pp. 215-230.*

Critical Evaluation

Is the research question clearly articulated?

Yes. The author primarily intends to explore the nature of three women's experience of breast cancer with a focus on body image issues. As part of this question, she also wants to explore whether massage, as a body-centered intervention, might be helpful as a means of helping the women adjust to a changed body image.

What assumptions underlie the study; what model or paradigm forms its theoretical basis?

This study is clearly relying upon assumptions common to the qualitative paradigm. In terms of its theoretical basis, the study is based on phenomenology in that it explores the nature of the participants' experience of their changed bodies following the loss of a breast, and of the massage intervention. It is not strictly speaking a phenomenological study because it does not seek out the essence of the experience. It is a descriptive study, and uses the technique of 'thick description.' Although the author's conclusions are grounded in the data presented, no theory is developed.

What are the researcher's qualifications, experience, and perspective?

Little information about the author's qualifications is presented. From the author information paragraph, the reader can determine that she is a nurse who works in a cancer research unit, and from the text, that she has some experience giving massage. It is not clear whether she has published other articles on this or on similar topics; no citations from previous studies authored by her are listed in the references. She does not appear to be endorsing any position about the use of massage for women struggling with an altered body image following mastectomy. Her interpretation of the study findings seems well supported by the data presented, and she also discusses the study's limitations.

What techniques and methods were used to ensure the integrity of the results as well as their validity and accuracy? Are the methods used in data collection and analysis described in sufficient detail?

The description of the study methodology is somewhat vague. Some purposeful sampling was employed, by asking oncologists and nurses to identify patients who appeared to be having difficulty adjusting to the loss of a breast and who could acknowledge this verbally. Other inclusion/exclusion criteria were set as well, although no rationale for their use is given. The author did attempt to avoid bias by having an associate conduct the post-intervention interview so that participants would not feel the need to please her. The massage intervention is not described in detail; the amount of time for the session is not given. Although interviews were taped and transcribed to ensure accuracy, the reader who is unfamiliar with the work of Lincoln & Guba is at a loss to understand exactly how the researcher proceeded in terms of the data analysis process. Triangulation of the data analysis, such as having more than one person reading, sorting, and coding the interviews to identify common themes in the women's experiences, would increase the accuracy and validity of the results. Jane's experience could be considered a negative case, of sorts.

Given the theoretical model and the purpose of the study, are the methods used appropriate?

This is a difficult question to answer. Certainly, a somewhat larger sample size with more features such as triangulation and a more highly defined theoretical approach such as grounded theory might have increased the applicability of the findings. Sampling to the point of redundancy, that is, continuing to identify and interview participants until no new information is forthcoming, would also have increased validity. One way to view this study is to look at it as a pilot study, with its stated purpose of exploring the participants' experience. The author justifies her sample size in terms of the limited resource of time, since she is providing the massage intervention. We can infer that money is also a limited resource, or else the sample size could have been increased by hiring another therapist to provide massage.

Are the results credible?

Given the previously stated limitations of the study, yes. The author has explored the research question, not quite as fully as we might have liked, but as well as possible under the practical limitations she faced. Certainly, the topic of body image in breast cancer is quite clinically relevant and the results of this study are meaningful, if only to raise awareness and sensitivity to these issues among other care providers, and provide some suggestions for additional ways to help patients.

Do the results justify the conclusions?

Yes, again given the stated limitations of the study. This study could also be a good source of pilot data for the development of a larger scale study exploring the same issue, or for a study evaluating the usefulness of massage in addressing body image distress.

One of the strengths of qualitative research is its reporting of raw data in the form of direct quotes from interviews. In this case, it may appear to some readers that there is a disparity between Jane's comments about her emotional response and the author's remarks about whether she may have been harmed. While the caution regarding the potential for massage to bring up difficult emotions prematurely is well taken, in Jane's case this seems a bit patronizing based on her choice to continue the treatments and her comment that she has "felt better since."

Can the results be generalized to other settings? Are they clinically meaningful?

The author states clearly that the results are not intended to be generalized. However, one can argue that this is a rich and useful study with a detailed description of clients' experience. The practitioner working with women who have had mastectomies would find valuable information in the study, both in understanding issues such clients may face, and in inferring ways that massage therapists may choose to interact with and treat them. It is a clinically meaningful study in terms of showing how massage can affect recipients on multiple levels.

Summary

Although the underlying assumptions, approaches, and methods used in qualitative health care research are quite different from those in quantitative research, its evaluation is similar. Qualitative research requires equal rigor in its design, conduct and analysis. Methodological flaws in any type of research are often related to practical and logistical issues, and the reader must judge these realistically. No study is perfect, whether qualitative or quantitative, and the informed reader should assess both the merits and flaws of a given study to determine its credibility.

References

1. Patton MQ. *Qualitative Evaluation and Research Methods*. Newbury Park, CA: Sage Publications, Inc.; 1990.

2. Glaser BG & Strauss AL. *The Discovery of Grounded Theory: Strategies for Qualitative Research*. Hawthorne, NY: Aldine; 1967.

3. Lincoln YS & Guba EG. *Naturalistic Inquiry*. Newbury Park, CA: Sage Publications, Inc.; 1985.

4. Greenhalgh T. *How to Read a Paper: The Basics of Evidence-based Medicine*. London: BMJ Publishing Group; 2001.

Exercise

1. Using PubMed or some other search engine, locate another article of interest to you that uses qualitative research methods, and evaluate it using the critique questions outlined in this chapter.

Glossary

Abstract

A concise summary of a research article, highlighting the objective, hypothesis, design, participants, setting, methods, results, and conclusion.

Analytic Study

Another term for a quantitative, experimental study.

Before-and-After Treatment Design

A research design comparing baseline measures taken before a treatment is given with those collected after.

Boolean Operators

The terms "and," "not," and "or" used to limit or to expand a search for reference citations in a database such as PubMed.

Case-control Study (Retrospective Study) (observation analysis retrospectively)

A type of observational study in which both the exposure(s) and outcome(s) have already occurred and are being analyzed retrospectively; often used to explore risk factors associated with chronic illness.

Citation

A reference to a journal article.

Clinical Trial

An experimental study where the researcher randomly assigns treatment(s) to groups of participants.

Cohort Study (follow up study) (longitudinal study) (prospective study)

A study in which a group is defined based on the presence or absence of an exposure in common, and then the participants are followed over time to observe who develops the outcome.

Co-intervention

Another procedure administered at the same time as the study intervention, occurring without the knowledge of the study investigator.

Compliance

Adherence to the study protocol.

Confounding Variable

A third variable that blurs the relationship between two other variables, making it appear that a spurious relationship exists.

Control Group (Comparison Group)

A group of study participants who do not receive the treatment being studied, or who do not have the exposure or outcome being evaluated; the group being used as a basis for comparison to the treatment group.

Culture

A particular way of defining the world, the relationship of a group to it and to each other, and accepted standards of behavior for the group. Culture is not limited to geographic location or ethnic heritage but can refer to any group of people who share a particular set of experiences, for example in organizations, schools, or workplaces.

Descriptive Study

A study that provides a record or description of events or activities.

Diffusion of Treatment

This is said to have occurred when study participants assigned to a control or comparison group seek out and obtain the active treatment.

Ecological Validity

The capacity of a study to accurately reflect the way a treatment is provided or implemented in clinical practice.

Experimental Study *subtype of explanatory study*

A study where the researcher manipulates events, for example by giving a treatment and then assessing its effects. *aka intervention or Tx study*

Explanatory Study

A study that seeks to explain a connection between events or variables. Explanatory studies can be further divided into observational and experimental studies.

Exposure

In epidemiology, the risk factor or treatment to which a study participant is subjected; analogous to independent variable in non-medical research.

External Validity

The capacity of a study to be generalized to other groups or clinical settings.

Falsification

The idea that science progresses best through demonstrating that a hypothesis is false.

Fields

Categories such as keywords, authors' names, journal titles, or textwords in an article that can be specified to limit or expand a database search.

Follow-up Study /cohort study / longitudinal study / prospective study

Another name for a cohort study.

Hypothesis

A highly specific statement that can be demonstrated to be true or false through the methodical gathering and analysis of empirical information or data.

Intention to Treat

Statistical analysis based on the total number of eligible participants originally enrolled in the study, instead of the number who completed the study.

Internal Validity

The capacity of a study to link cause and effect.

Intervention Study

Another term for an experimental or treatment study.

Iterative

Describes a process of repeated development or refinement, going through several cycles.

Letters to the Editor

A feature of a journal where readers write in response to previously published articles.

Literature Review

A critique of previous research studies on a particular topic.

Longitudinal Study / cohort study / follow up study / perspective study

Another name for a cohort study.

Margin of Error

The estimated amount of possible statistical error in a survey's results, usually expressed as a range, such as "plus or minus 3%."

Mean

The arithmetical average; the sum of a group of scores divided by the number of scores.

Nonspecific Response

A more accurate term for the placebo response, which is a positive response to an inactive substance or sham treatment; sometimes used to reflect the possibility that positive clinical outcomes may be in response to factors like expectations, beliefs, and attitudes.

Observational Study *subtype of explanatory study*

A study that explains a connection between naturally occurring events, such as exposure to a risk factor and subsequent development of an outcome, without manipulating those events.

Outcome

Any clinical endpoint of interest.

Prospective Study *cohort, longitudinal, follow up.*

Another name for a cohort or longitudinal study.

Protocol

The step by step description of concrete procedures to be carried out during a research study.

Publication Bias

The tendency for journals to publish articles with only positive findings.

✳ Qualitative Methods

Research methods that rely on the collection and analysis of word-based experiential and observational data, instead of numbers.

Quantitative Methods *analytic*

Research methods based on the collection and analysis of numerical data.

Random Assignment

Assignment of study participants to group based on a random process, such as computer-generated tables of numbers.

Randomized Controlled Trial (RCT) *40+ <40 = pilot study*

A clinical trial whose participants have been randomly allocated to treatment and control groups; considered the 'gold standard' of quantitative research.

Range

The difference between the highest and lowest scores of an outcome measure.

Reactivity Issues

The ways in which the responses of study participants are influenced by the obtrusiveness of their being observed or measured during the course of the study.

Recall Bias

The tendency of study participants to distort historical information because of faulty memory or a desire to please or impress the interviewer, resulting in inaccurate data.

Regression to the Mean

The tendency for extreme values of a baseline measure to become closer to the average upon repeated measurement.

Reproducibility

The capacity of the study to be replicated by another investigator or in another setting.

Retrospective Study *case control study*

Another name for a case-control study.

Sample

The way in which cases from a population are selected to be representative of the entire population; also used as a noun to refer to the selected subset.

Search Strategy

Search terms used to retrieve articles on a particular topic.

Standard Deviation

A measure of the variability or spread of scores around the mean.

Statistical Significance

Evidence that the results of a study are not due to chance or random error.

Sources of Bias

Elements of a research design or procedures that introduce systematic error into the measurement of an outcome.

Test-Retest Reliability

Evidence of the stability of the test or instrument used to measure an abstract concept (e.g. anxiety) over time.

Triangulation

Use of more than one method or strategy of data collection or analysis in order to increase the validity/reliability of a qualitative study.

Type I Error

Statistical significance mistakenly based on random error, leading to the conclusion that an effect is present when in truth it is not.

Type II Error

Lack of statistical significance despite the presence of a true effect.

Index

An italic *f* following a page number indicates the presence of a Figure.

abstract, 26, 60–62
· evaluation of, 84, 105, 122
· narrative, 122
· standardized, 61, 122
allocation of participants, 54–55
Alternative Health News Online, 36
Alternative Medicine Review, 36
alternative therapies
  See complementary, alternative therapies
Alternative Therapies in Health and Medicine, 35
American Massage Therapy Association, 2, 21
· Foundation, 36, 37
analysis of covariance (ANCOVA), 55, 88, 107
analysis of variance (ANOVA), 88
analytical study, 48
anecdote, 46, 56*f*
attrition of participants, 16, 50, 55–56, 90, 123–24
author and article information, 60, 77–78

Ball, Don, 47
baseline measurement, 15
before-and-after treatment design, 45*f*, 51–52, 56*f*
best evidence synthesis, 43
bias, source(s) of, 14
· acknowledgement of, 50
· in case-control studies, 49

· cultural, 11
· in eligibility criteria, 54
· gauging of, 63
· lack of compliance as, 55
· neutrality bias, 131
· publication bias, 42
· recall bias, 50
· sampling bias, 86
· selection bias, 16, 54
· selective attrition as, 55
bibliographic reference software, 31
blinding, 18–19, 52, 86, 107, 122
· double-blind randomized clinical trial, 13, 52
· with peer reviews, 84, 105
· single and double, 18, 86
Boolean operators, 30
British Medical Journal, 35

Campbell, DT, 8, 14
Canada Institute for Scientific and Technical Information (CISTI), 35
case-control studies, 45*f*, 48, 49–50, 51, 56*f*
case report, 56*f*
cases (in study), 49
case series, 45*f*, 46, 56*f*
case studies, 45*f*, 46
Cassidy, Claire, 21
categorical data, 88*f*
cause and effect relationship, 14, 44, 56*f*
Centers for Disease Control, 46
Centralised Information Service for Complementary Medicine (CISCOM), 36
chi square test (χ^2), 88

citations, 26
· in articles, 75, 78, 92–93
· in PubMed, 27
clinical significance (of study), 92, 109–10, 125, 149
clinical trials, 45*f*, 51, 52–56, 56*f*
· characteristics of, 53–56
· websites for, 35
ClinicalTrials.gov (website), 35
Cochrane Collaboration, 42–43
cohort studies, 45*f*, 48, 50–51, 56*f*
co-interventions, 55
comparison group. *See* control group
complementary, alternative therapies
· before-and-after treatment designs, 51
· ecological validity, 86
· individualized treatment, 21
· model fit validity, 21–22
· online resources for, 36
· qualitative research methods, 47, 86
· *See also* massage therapy research
compliance, 55
Computerized Index to Nursing and Allied Health Literature (CINAHL), 27
Computer Retrieval of Information on Scientific Projects (CRISP), 37
computers
· access to, 26
· bibliographic software, 31
· cookies, 27
· statistical software, 89
conclusion (of article)
  See discussion or conclusion
confound, 14, 47

confounding variables, 55
consistency (in qualitative study), 130–31
Consortium for Chiropractic Research, 36
control group (comparison group, placebo group), 86, 107, 122, 123
· in before-and-after treatment designs, 52, 56*f*
· in case-control studies, 49
· random assignment to, 17–18, 86
· randomized controlled trial (RTC),13, 52, 56*f*, 96
· to rule out maturation, 15
· use of placebo with, 19–20
· *See also* participants
controlled vocabulary, 29
Cook, TD, 8, 14
cookies (tags), 27
correlational studies, 45*f*, 46–47, 56*f*
Cronbach, Lee, 10
crossover design, 19–20
cross-sectional studies, 45*f*, 48–49, 51, 56*f*
culture, 129–30

data
· analysis of, 108, 124
· consistency with conclusions, 91
· interval *vs.* categorical, 88*f*
· in qualitative studies, 131–2, 148
· subjective, 52
databases, reference, 26, 35–37, 41
· searching outside of, 42
degrees of freedom (DF), 90–91
demographic data, 18, 48–49, 68, 90
· baseline, 54
· and random assignment, 55, 64, 68
descriptive statistics, 87–88, 107, 123
descriptive studies, 44, 45*f*, 46–47
diffusion of treatment, 18
discussion or conclusion (of article), 60, 75–77, 91–92, 108–10, 124–25
dissertations, 42
double blind study, 13, 18, 86

ecological validity, 86
effect size, 91, 108
eligibility criteria, 54
EMBASE, 27
empiricism, 8–9

epidemiological research, 44
ethical issues
· with experimental studies, 51
· with placebos and control groups, 18
· with sham treatments, 21
ethics review committee, 18
ethnography, 129–30
evaluation (of research), 13–22, 40
· of before-and-after treatment designs, 52
· of case studies, case series, 46
· of methodology, 63–64
· of a qualitative study, 132, 147–9
· of a quantitative study, 84–93, 104
· of a references list, 78
evidence-based medicine, 9, 42–43
experimental population, 53
experimental studies, 44–57, 45*f*, 51–52
explanatory studies, 44, 45*f*, 48–56
exposure, 44, 47, 52, 56
· time of measurement, 48, 49
external validity, 13–14

falsification, 10
Field, Tiffany, 2, 41
fields (in citation), 26
final statistic, 90–91
follow-up studies, 50
FreeMedicalJournals.com, 36
funding sources (for research), 11, 60, 77

generalizability, 130
graphs, 89–90, 108, 123
Greiner, David, 89
grounded theory, 129
Guba, EG, 130, 148

healing (therapeutic) relationship, 21, 47
HealthStar, 27
history (event in a study), 14
history (of a search), 30*f*
Hotelling's T2, 89
hypotheses, 9, 45*f*, 85
· in before-and-after treatment designs, 52
· case study as basis for, 46
· and falsification, 10

· and outcome measures, 91, 107, 123
· testing with correlational studies, 47
· and treatment procedure, 107, 123
· validation of, 10

independent variable, 88
inferential statistics, 88–89, 107, 123, 124
Institutional Review Boards, 18
instrumentation, 15
intention to treat, 56
internal validity, 14
· and random assignment, 86
· threats to, 14–16
· and weighting methods, 42, 43
International Chiropractic Online Network, 36
interval data, 88*f*
intervention studies, 52, 86–87
· evaluation of, 96, 105–10, 122–6
introduction (of article), 62–63, 85, 105–6, 122

Jonas, Wayne, 51
journal articles
evaluation of quantitative study, 84–93
to locate, 26, 29–37
to order from PubMed, 33–34
peer review of, 84
published online, 35–37
relevance and context of, 85, 105, 122
journal articles: sections of, 60
· abstract, 26, 60–2, 84, 105, 122
· author and article information, 60, 77–78
· discussion or conclusion, 60, 75–7, 91–2, 108–10, 124–5
· introduction, 60, 62–63, 85, 105–6, 122
· methods and procedures, 60, 63–68, 85–89, 106–7, 122–23
· references, 41, 60, 78–80, 92–93, 110, 125
· results, 60, 68–74, 89–91, 108, 123–24
Journal of the American Medical Association, The, 3, 35
journals
· letters to editor in, 40